LOST
LONG ISLAND

LOST
LONG ISLAND

RICHARD PANCHYK

THE
History
PRESS

Published by The History Press
Charleston, SC
www.historypress.com

First published 2024

Manufactured in the United States

ISBN 9781467155205

Library of Congress Control Number: 2023945813

CONTENTS

ACKNOWLEDGEMENTS

Thanks to Banks and all the staff at The History Press for their work on making this book a reality. I am also thankful for all those who have worked so hard in recent years to digitize thousands of old newspapers, books, and photographs, which are an invaluable resource. And a very special thanks to Miranda for all her ideas and suggestions to help make this book better.

IMAGE CREDITS

INTRODUCTION

I n one interesting way, Long Island itself is lost.

It may be the only island on earth where more than half the people living on it do not even acknowledge the fact that they live on it! It is indeed an actual geographical, physical island that spans 118 miles in length, from Bay Ridge to Montauk, from Astoria to Orient Point, but if someone says they are from Long Island, we know that they mean only either Nassau or Suffolk County. If you are one of the nearly five million people from Queens or Brooklyn, you'd say you live in those boroughs or New York City, but you wouldn't say you live on Long Island because socially and politically, you don't, even though geographically and physically, you do.

It was not always like this. Fascinatingly, the Long Island disassociation is in fact a fairly recent identity phenomenon.

Before Queens and Brooklyn were part of New York City, of course, their identities were firmly connected to Long Island, and with good reason. For hundreds of years, the city was Manhattan only, and everything located on that island to its east was considered part of Long Island. The westernmost point in Queens was even named Long Island City. Back then, Queens County even included what is today's Nassau County. Maps of the time would include the words "Long Island" whether showing Flushing or Setauket. The identity of Long Island as a place was so strong that letters sent to locations on the island might not have even included the words "New York" in the address, just the town name and "L.I. or "Long Island," and that was enough for it to be delivered.

A 1907 postcard is simply addressed to "Albert Herzog, Greenport, Long Island."

Even after Brooklyn and western Queens split away to join with Manhattan in 1898 and become a part of New York City, the Long Island identity continued. For example, a history book published one year after, in 1899, was titled *History of the Town of Flushing, Long Island, New York*. Even into the 1940s and 1950s, if you addressed a letter to someone living anywhere on physical Long Island, you'd likely still include the "L.I." A late 1950s postcard for the Skyway Motel across from LaGuardia Airport gave its address as "Jackson Heights, Queens, L.I., N.Y."

With the introduction of zip codes in 1963 came a more standardized way of addressing mail—city, state, and zip code. There was no room for additional identifiers. By the early 1970s, as everyone finally fell in line and adopted zip codes, the use of "L.I." or "Long Island" in addresses vanished, and so did the Long Island identity for Queens and Brooklyn, thus strengthening the Long Island identity for the remainder.

In keeping with the above, this book features twenty-one stories of lost Nassau and Suffolk locations, phenomena, people, and activities—covering everything from glaciers to auto racing, from whaling to presidents. Lost places in Queens and Brooklyn will have to be the subject for another book. For now, enjoy the ride through lost Long Island!

Chapter 1

LOST BEGINNINGS

The Long Island phenomenon that has been "lost" for the longest time is in fact the very thing that shaped its geography and physical appearance the most, thousands of years ago—glaciers! Long Island's geography was uniquely influenced by advancing and retreating glaciers starting about nineteen thousand years ago.

Long Island is unique because upon it lies the Terminal Moraine, the point of farthest advance of the glaciers during the last ice age in North America. The lightly hilly northern section of the island was heavily shaped by the glacial advance and retreat.

Many of the chapters of this book cover topics that are closely linked to the glacier-influenced geography, from farms to mansions, from polo to aviation. The beaches of the north shore are rocky and sometimes accessible via a steep drop-off in the land, whereas the south shore's waterfront tends to be on marshy flat land. The outwash from the melting and retreating glaciers was sandy material that was deposited, pushed forward ahead of the glaciers.

Though the glaciers themselves are long lost, the gifts they left behind are not. Some of the geological remainders left by the retreating glaciers were thousands of boulders of various sizes, known as "glacial erratics." These boulders were carried along by the ice hundreds of miles, from points north down to Long Island, and then deposited as the ice melted and retreated. Those living in the northern half of the island are probably familiar with these large rocks that vary in size from a foot or two in diameter to more than a dozen feet wide.

A glacial boulder of gneiss on the beach near Riverhead, 1917.

Some Long Island boulders are even somewhat famous, such as Shelter Rock, supposedly the largest boulder in New York State, located just off the appropriately named Shelter Rock Road in Manhasset. Weighing an estimated 1,800 tons, Shelter Rock is fifty-five feet high by forty feet wide by sixteen feet deep. It was already about five hundred million years old when a large glacier brought this large metamorphic present to Long Island. Another famous boulder is Council Rock in Oyster Bay, the site where in 1672 the father of the Quaker movement, George Fox, arrived from England to Oyster Bay and preached to a crowd in the woods just west of town.

There is also a forty-five-ton rock memorial to the martyred Revolutionary War Patriot Nathan Hale and the marker on the summit of Jayne's Hill (highest point on Long Island) in Huntington. Many communities on the north shore have memorial boulders to commemorate important events, places, or people. The Sands Point Giant, on a private estate, is forty by forty by seventeen feet. Not all boulders are so large; many homeowners on the island have small boulders in their backyards. Glacial boulders can even be seen way out at Montauk, where they litter the waterfront.

Kettle ponds or small lakes formed by the glaciers are also still evident around the island, in places such as the Muttontown Preserve in Nassau County. They were formed when pieces of glacier broke off and then were partially buried and slowly melted. At 234 acres, Lake Ronkonkoma in Suffolk is the largest of the island's kettle lakes. Though only 14.5 feet deep on average, it has a low spot of 90 feet deep. Kettle ponds are also found on private land; a lavish Bridgehampton estate was being offered for sale in 2023 for $50 million, containing 60 acres of land and three kettle ponds stocked with bass.

Another interesting feature formed by the glacial outwash was the Hempstead Plains, the largest prairie east of the Mississippi River. This forty-thousand-acre grassland (before nineteenth-century development) was a direct result of the effect of the advancing and retreating ice sheets.

An early American colonist named Daniel Denton, who published a book describing his impressions of New York in 1670, wrote of the Hempstead Plains: "Toward the middle of Long Island lyeth a plain, sixteen miles long and four broad, upon which plain grows very fine grass, that makes excellent good hay, and is very good pasture for sheep and other cattle; where you shall find neither stick nor stone to hinder the horses' heels or endanger them in their races."

What did the Hempstead Plains look like in the mid-nineteenth century? Winslow C. Watson wrote in his 1860 book titled *The Plains of Long Island*:

> *Unoccupied, uncultivated, without enclosures,* [the plains] *present to the eye a wide expanse, clothed in rich and beautiful verdure. This vast surface is almost perfectly level, interrupted by slight undulations, and stretching from the ridge towards the ocean, by a declination so gradual as to be imperceptible. Scarcely a bush or tree interrupts the view. Nature formed it*

Glacial outwash plain near New Hyde Park, looking north to the terminal moraine, 1917.

a broad, upland meadow. Its appearance recalls at once the memory of a Western prairie, and the herds of cattle ranging over it, which fancy may readily conceive to be the Buffalo, do not lessen the similitude.

Over the centuries, more and more of the Hempstead Plains were developed. At the time of Watson's book, he claimed the Hempstead Plains had decreased in size by 30 percent from their original expanse. The size of the virgin prairie was soon to be reduced even more, for less than ten years later in 1869, the wealthy Alexander T. Stewart purchased 7,170 acres of prairie from the Town of Hempstead for fifty-five dollars an acre and turned much of that land into Garden City over the next few years.

There are three pieces of Hempstead Plains prairie that are left today. One is adjacent to Nassau Community College; another is between the Meadowbrook Parkway and the Marriott Hotel; and the third is located on the northern edge of the Red Course at Eisenhower Park. Some of the hundreds of grasses and plants that grow on the Hempstead Plains remnants include big bluestem, little bluestem, Indian grass, switchgrass rush, wild indigo, Canada cinquefoil, gray goldenrod, early goldenrod, butterfly-weed, stargrass, fringed violet, and stiff-leaf aster.

Not too long after the retreat of the glaciers, Native Americans arrived from the west and settled across Long Island from what is now Brooklyn all the way to Montauk, but especially in locations along the north and south shores and near rivers and bays, where the water was nearby and fish were plentiful. There were thirteen Algonquin tribes that populated the island in prehistoric times, from west to east: the Canarsie, Rockaway, Merrick, Massapequa, Matinecock, Nissaquogue, Setauket, Corchaugs, Secatogue, Unkechaug, Shinnecock, Montaukett, and Manhanset. They grew corn and vegetables and enjoyed the plentiful deer along with fish and shellfish. By the time Europeans arrived in the Long Island area in the early 1600s, Native Americans had already been there for thousands of years, a total population of over ten thousand people living off the land and sea. Artifacts of their early existence are still being found at many locations. This author, while in college, participated in archaeological excavations at Leeds Pond in Manhasset, where shell debris and stone tool remains were discovered.

As English and Dutch settlers arrived, they eagerly purchased land from the Natives. The purchase of land in present-day Huntington in 1653 comprised about six square miles; the Natives received six coats, six bottles, six hatchets, six shovels, ten knives, six fathom wampum, thirty awl blades, and thirty needles. A 30,720-acre purchase of East Hampton land netted the

Natives twenty coats, twenty-four looking glasses, twenty-four hoes, twenty-four hatchets, twenty-four knives, and one hundred awl blades. A purchase of 20,000 acres of Oyster Bay land was made for six coats, six kettles, six fathom of wampum, six hoes, six hatchets, three pairs of stockings, thirty awl blades, twenty knives, and three shirts. The Native Americans of Long Island used wampum (perforated shells the size of beads) as their form of money, and for a time, the Dutch and English accepted and used this money themselves, with three black beads or six white beads equal to one penny in value. At times, the two groups got along well, but other times the Europeans were wary of the Indigenous peoples and passed laws against selling weapons or alcohol to them.

Ultimately, diseases introduced by the Europeans and a general intolerance of Native American presence near the colonial settlements marginalized and decimated the Native population such that by the end of the seventeenth century, it was largely gone. Much of the pre-contact and early post-contact Native history has been lost; what is left is mostly biased seventeenth-century European deeds and purchase records and accounts of the Indigenous people. The Montauk tribe was reduced to 192 people by 1761, and by 1838, the number was down to 30 people. Though the Native population was severely reduced, it never vanished completely; some tribes did largely vanish, but others continued to exist, notably the Shinnecocks. In 1884, a photograph was taken with the handwritten caption "The last

Shinnecock tribe members on Long Island, 1884.

of the Shinnecock Indians, L.I., N.Y.," yet the tribe survives to this day, experiencing a recent resurgence with the official recognition by the U.S. government in 2010 of the Shinnecock Indian Nation. The Shinnecocks have a nine-hundred-acre tribal reservation adjacent to Shinnecock Bay in Suffolk County, with about 800 members living on the property and another 800 members living off-reservation.

Native American influence also lives on in countless Long Island place names such as Amagansett, Cutchogue, Mattituck, Nissequogue, Montauk, Speonk, Setauket, Ronkonkoma, Patchogue, Wantagh, and Massapequa, to name just a few. Many of these names were standardized from a wide variety of spellings; for example, Aquebogue was mentioned in an 1648 deed between Natives and Europeans as Ocquebauck, but it was also referred to as Occabock, Occobauk, Agabake, and Hauquebaug in the seventeenth century. All the names mean the same thing: "at the head of the bay," which describes the village's location perfectly. One of the places where Native American presence is celebrated and studied is the Garvies Point Preserve, a science museum in Glen Cove that has numerous artifacts on display and offers programs to teach schoolkids about pre-contact Native life.

Though Long Island's beginnings are in the distant past, they served as a precursor to everything that has transpired since. The glaciers shaped the island's very geography, on which the Native peoples flourished for thousands of years before the Europeans arrived.

Chapter 2

LOST QUAKER ABOLITIONISTS

Quakers, aka the Religious Society of Friends, are a religious group that originated in mid-seventeenth-century England and first came to America shortly after that. Their two main principles, according to their website, are: 1) all people are capable of directly experiencing the divine nature of the universe (every person is known by God and can know God in a direct relationship), and 2) a belief in continued divine revelation. Many of the Quakers who came here were just looking for religious freedom that the colonies seemed to promise. However, they were met with skepticism and animosity, at times putting their very safety in jeopardy. Though Pennsylvania is known as the "Quaker State," many Quakers chose to settle on Long Island.

Stories from the annals of Long Island's history show how badly Quakers were treated in the early days of their presence here. In March 1658, Southold Quaker Humphrey Norton was arrested and sent to the general court in New Haven, Connecticut. The list of charges he was tried for included slander against a pastor, seducing people away from their religions, trying to spread heretical opinions, using blasphemous language, attempting to circumvent the authority of the government, and instigating rebellion and disorder with boisterous language and unseemly conduct. His conviction was that of a fine of twenty pounds along with a sentence of being severely whipped and being branded with an *H* on his hand.

In 1660, Mary Wright of Oyster Bay was arrested for being a witch and selling herself to Satan. Most peculiar was that the biggest piece of evidence against her was that she was a poor old ignorant woman with no friends. The townspeople agreed this was a serious matter to be accused of witchcraft; however, they were not equipped to handle a case like this, as they were unfamiliar with the means of investigating and judging suspected witches. Instead, they sent her away to the general court of Massachusetts, where they were notorious for the "accurate" questioning and sentencing of witches. Mary was acquitted of the charges of witchcraft after a grueling process. Unfortunately, her fate was sealed when she was tried and found guilty instead of being a Quaker. This, a quite serious charge in itself, resulted in her being sentenced to banishment.

By the eighteenth century, as early superstitions and fears faded away, the Quakers had become much more accepted and in many cases were an integral part of the commercial and political landscape of their towns. Quakers were an especially large part of the population in certain towns on Long Island, including Jericho and Westbury, for example. They built meetinghouses in numerous locations around which their members were concentrated, including Westbury, Jericho, Bethpage, Manhasset, Locust Valley, Flushing, St. James, Shelter Island Heights, and Peconic Bay (all of which still exist).

In an ironic and wonderful historical twist, Quakers went from being persecuted to helping stop persecution of others. The Quakers were very progressive in their ideas about the treatment of African Americans. In 1671, Quaker founder George Fox and other fellow Quakers visited Barbados and saw and met with slaves. He wrote: "I desired also that they would cause their overseers to deal mildly and gently with their negroes, and not use cruelty towards them…and that, after certain years of servitude, they should make them free." In 1675, another Quaker, William Edmondson, visited Barbados and said: "Did not God make us all of one mould?…Christ's command is, to do to others as we would have them do to us; and which of you would have the blacks, or others, to make you their slaves, without hope or expectation of freedom or liberty?"

One of the earliest Quaker abolitionists in the American colonies was John Woolman of New Jersey, who published an essay protesting slavery in 1754. Before anyone else was even considering the emancipation of slaves, the Quakers were already doing it. During the 1770s, nearly ninety years before President Abraham Lincoln would sign the Emancipation Proclamation, the Quakers of Westbury Meeting and elsewhere on Long Island began to free their slaves, filling out and registering "manumission papers" that read:

Be it Known to all men by these presents that I (name), of (place), in Queens County, and province of New York do by these presents fully freely and voluntarily manumit and set free my Negro man named (name) fully and freely acquitted and Discharged from me and my heirs Executor and Administrators forever, and that the Said Negro named (name), Shall and may as far as in my power Exercise and enjoy his freedom in all Respects, to all Intents and purposes Whatsoever.

The Westbury Meeting registered ninety manumission papers in 1776 and 1777 alone. A Quaker named Phebe Dodge set her slave Rachel free in 1776. Thomas Seaman had bought a slave as a young man but was not pleased with him and so sold the slave. Later, when the Quakers decided to make a stand against slavery and began to free their slaves, Seaman bought that same slave back solely in order to free him.

One of the country's earliest and most vocal abolitionists was Elias Hicks, who moved to Jericho (a largely Quaker settlement) from Hempstead after his marriage to Jemima Seaman in 1771, into a house built by his in-laws. It was not long after moving to Jericho that he flocked to ministry. He helped

The Quaker meetinghouse in Jericho dates to 1788.

build the Jericho meetinghouse and spoke at meetings, which eventually led to the spreading of the word of antislavery. He was responsible for helping free 154 Quaker-owned slaves.

All of Westbury's Quaker-owned slaves were freed by 1799. Hicks was not satisfied with that. He wanted to see all slaves freed unconditionally, and so his quest continued. Inspired by his passion and drive for the abolishment of slavery, Hicks traveled and gave many lectures that assisted in the spreading of his abolitionist views. He used blunt statements to make his points. In one of his lectures, he proclaimed:

> We are on a level with all the rest of God's creatures. We are not better for being white than others for being black; and we have no more right to oppress the blacks because they are black than they have to oppress us because we are white. Therefore, every one who oppresses his colored brother or sister is a tyrant upon the earth; and every one who strengthens the hand of an oppressor is a tyrant upon earth.

In 1811, Hicks published an antislavery essay that posed various questions upon the community to continue the conversation about slavery and the false implications of slaves. In *Observations on the Slavery of Africans and Their Descendants and on the Use of the Produce of Their Labor*, Hicks made a strong case for the abolition of slavery through a series of questions and answers. His first question set a powerful tone for the logic he employed in the booklet:

> *Query 1. Were not the people of Africa, at the time when the Europeans first visited their coasts, a free people, possessed of the same natural and unalienable rights, as the people of any other nation?*
>
> *Answer. They certainly were: for, when the Europeans, whether by fraud or force, or by purchase from those who had stolen or taken them prisoners in war, became possessed of a number of the people of Africa, and by violence reduced them to the wretched and degraded state of Slaves.*

In Query 5, Hicks asked: "Does it lessen the criminality and wickedness of reducing our fellow creatures to the abject state of slavery, and continuing them therein, because the practice is tolerated by the laws of the country we live in?" and his answer begins, "No! by no means. Because, every rational creature knows, or ought to know, that no laws of men or nations, can alter the nature of immutable justice."

In Query 9, Hicks proposed a solution to the slavery issue in his home state. "What measures can be adopted by the Legislature and citizens of New York, in order to exculpate themselves from the guilt of that atrocious crime of holding the Africans and their descendants so long in slavery?" With the answer, "The least that can be done…would be to declare freedom to every slave in the state, and to make provision by law for the education of all minors that are in a state of slavery."

Thanks to pressure from Hicks and his fellow Long Island Quakers, New York State had partially freed its slaves in 1799, passing a law that stated children born of slave mothers after July 4 of that year would be free when they reached the age of twenty-five for women and twenty-eight for men. This law was followed by the Gradual Manumission Act of 1817, which stated that all slaves would be free on July 4, 1827. But the struggle was not over. Slavery continued elsewhere, especially in the southern states. Long Island's Quakers became widely known for their antislavery views. In 1849, abolitionist Frederick Douglass visited Westbury and stayed with the Quaker Post family.

Sometimes slaves escaped their masters and sought freedom, and Long Island's Quakers were eager to help. Thus was born the Underground Railroad, a series of "safe" houses often with secret rooms where runaway slaves could be sheltered until being shuttled to their next stop on their way to Connecticut and eventually to Canada where they'd be safe.

The home of Elias Hicks's son-in-law, Valentine Hicks, was a stop on the legendary Underground Railroad. Located in Jericho, this building would become the Maine Maid Inn, a popular restaurant for decades. Another stop was the home of Rachel Hicks on Post Road in Old Westbury.

In 1850, Congress passed the Fugitive Slave Act, which required that slaves be returned to their owners, even if they had reached a free state such as New York. It was a dangerous business—the Fugitive Slave Act set the punishment for helping, harboring, or concealing a runaway slave at up to $1,000 or six months in prison. The law also set out fees for those who helped capture slaves. The Quakers were not deterred in their desire to help. With the end of the Civil War in 1865, all slaves in the reunited country were finally free.

As the nineteenth century progressed, numerous Quaker estates were purchased by wealthy Manhattanites and others who would create the Gold Coast (see chapters 5 and 6). For example, the Phipps estate, which is now Old Westbury Gardens, was formerly a Quaker farm. Similarly, the land purchased by "the Babe Ruth of Polo" Thomas Hitchcock, in

The building formerly known as the Maine Maid Inn belonged to Valentine Hicks and was a stop on the Underground Railroad.

Old Westbury in the 1890s, was previously an eighteenth-century Quaker homestead (the property is now the Diocese of Rockville Centre's newly opened Queen of Peace Cemetery).

A 1987 Nassau County Museum exhibit on Long Island Quaker history displayed over three hundred documents, paintings and pieces of furniture and clothing telling the story of Quaker life. As of 2017, there were about seventy-six thousand Quakers in the United States, representing about a third of the world population of Quakers (for comparison, there are over fifty million Catholics in the United States today). A walk through Long Island's Quaker cemeteries reveals so many of the old Quaker names: Valentine, Willett, Post, Hicks, Jackson, Seaman, Albertson, Cocks, Carle, Conklin, and Willis. These are not only some of the oldest families on Long Island, but they are also some of the most prominent. Many local and national elected leaders were members of these families, including William Willets Cocks (1861–1932), who served in the House of Representatives from 1905 to 1911, and his brother Frederick Cocks Hicks (1872–1925), who served in the House from 1915 to 1921 (both buried in the Westbury Friends Cemetery). Who were some other famous Quakers? William Penn, after whom Pennsylvania is named; John Cadbury, founder of the famous chocolate company; Herbert Hoover, the thirty-first U.S.

president; Richard Nixon, the thirty-seventh U.S. president; and James Dean, the iconic actor.

Quakers are still around today on Long Island. Today they have spread from the several main towns where they used to be concentrated and seemingly meld in with all the other faiths and groups on Long Island. They are no longer separated out by history as Quakers but are just a vibrant part of their communities who happen to belong to a unique and special faith with centuries-old roots on Long Island—and a unique role in helping free New York's slaves and as part of the Underground Railroad, assisting runaway slaves from elsewhere.

Chapter 3

LOST FARMING

Current-day Suffolk County is well known for its farm-fresh produce of all kinds. Families go there for apple, peach, and pumpkin picking and to enjoy the bounty of its dozens of farmstands that prosper from spring through autumn, offering fresh corn and tomatoes, among many other vegetables. But beyond catering to visitors, Suffolk farms produce fruit and vegetables on a much larger scale, selling their crops to the Greater New York City metropolitan area and beyond. As of 2019, Suffolk County still ranked fourth in farm sales among all New York State counties.

Nassau County too used to be farming paradise, but that changed quickly during the twentieth century. Farming in Nassau County is largely gone; there are only three working farms in the entire county as of 2023: Youngs Farm and Rottkamp Farm in Brookville and Meyer's Farm in Woodbury. And though Youngs Farm sells plenty of produce, some of it comes not from their own fields but from Suffolk County farms. This poses the questions: how and why did this happen?

In the nineteenth century, Long Island was largely farmland. Outside of a few villages and town centers, the surrounding areas were farms. The island's population was a local economy that relied on local growers to feed them, but these farms also fed people in nearby New York City as well. In 1819, the first agricultural fair in the area was held, with a few more in the following years. The fair led a nomadic existence during its first two decades, moving around between locations such as Flushing, Hempstead, and Jamaica. The Queens County Agricultural Society (Queens County then included what is now Nassau County) was formed in 1841 and held its first fair in 1842 in the yard of a hotel in the village of Hempstead. By the 1860s, the fair had moved to Mineola, where for over eighty years it was an annual fixture for farmers to meet and show off all things agricultural.

The agricultural situation did not change too much by the late nineteenth century, except for a few of the farms that were located on the periphery of the old villages of Long Island, places such as Westbury, where the "center of town" was a stretch that was a few blocks long and wide. Just a few hundred feet away in any direction from downtown were farms. Around the turn of the twentieth century, as the village and many others like it grew in size and importance, the immediately outlying small farms (often dairy farms) were sold and developed to build private homes as these villages expanded. If you live on Long Island, chances are good that where your dwelling stands used to be a farm.

Farms disappeared first in northern Nassau County because there was another force at play in that area between about 1890 and 1930—the influx of millionaires from New York City and other locations relocating to construct colossal mansions in what would be known as the Gold Coast.

Two women working with a plow on a farm at the New York State Agricultural College at Farmingdale, April 1917.

The slightly hilly, somewhat wooded areas that are north of Westbury and Carle Place were perfect for the construction of their new homes. The area was close enough to the Hempstead Plains, where the Meadowbrook Club offered polo and the nearby airfields offered the novel spectacle of flight. A great many of these wealthy businessmen purchased Quaker farms and converted these bucolic properties into lavishly landscaped and appointed estates crowned by mansions with dozens of rooms. Sometimes, a Quaker building or two remained if the new owners deemed them charming or useful enough. In the case of Old Westbury Gardens, the "cottage" and nearby barn (now used for special events) were some of those original Quaker farm buildings. When star polo player and horse trainer Thomas Hitchcock bought property in Old Westbury, he modernized an existing eighteenth-century Quaker homestead into a nineteenth-century mansion. This land was since purchased by the Diocese of Rockville Centre and has been converted to a new Catholic cemetery. By the 1920s, there was almost no farmland left in the Gold Coast area; one parcel after another was being used for one-hundred-acre (and more) estates.

Things soon changed elsewhere in Nassau County because real estate is largely a numbers game. Property use is wildly dependent on cost-effectiveness; it is market-based factors that determine the future of property. Farmland will remain farmland so long as it is economically feasible—taxes are low enough, production and produce prices are high enough and demand for the land itself is low enough.

However, it deserves to be mentioned that throughout the early twentieth century, farming was still huge in central Nassau County. In fact, as of 1929, there were more acres of corn planted in Nassau than Suffolk. The same was true for carrots, lettuce, spinach, and peas. In 1929, Nassau County farmers produced 294,000 dozen eggs and 663,780 gallons of milk. Poultry and dairy were not the only booming harvests in Nassau throughout the twentieth century. The boom in potato crops throughout Nassau County in the mid-twentieth century made them the dominant crop in that area of Long Island. This may seem odd considering that if you go to your local supermarket now, chances are the potatoes you buy will come from either Maine or Idaho.

By 1909, fifteen thousand acres on Long Island were devoted to potato growing, with a yield of two hundred bushels per acre, as compared to one hundred bushels per acre elsewhere in the state of New York. Long Island potatoes were considered the highest quality, with the crop bringing the highest wholesale price of any potatoes in the country—three cents per pound.

Fred Franklin about to leave to market with a truck full of Long Island potatoes from Wantagh.

Long Island Potato Tours started around 1918, offering upstate New York farmers a chance to see Long Island's potato fields. That year, the tour lasted three days and saw about eighty Suffolk County farmers showing the thirty-five upstate visitors around the various farms. In 1928, the Potato Tour ran three days and featured fifty automobiles in procession visiting the various potato fields on the island. The tour also visited the Riverhead Experiment Station, studying fertilizer tests.

Potatoes began to outnumber other crops, which were starting to decrease in numbers. For example, corn production in Nassau County went down from 403,880 bushels in 1899 to 7,612 bushels in 1929.

Vintage 1939 and 1946 maps of Nassau County show dozens of farm plots in the eastern central part of the county (Hicksville, Plainedge, Island Trees, Jerusalem area). Typically, in the twenty- to sixty-acre size range, many of the names are Polish or German in origin: Gerhard, Podsiadlo, Schabehorn, Hartmann, Abramowski, Kroemer, Sauer, Kraus. Soon after, however, these and other Nassau County potato farms were obtained for residential purposes, including and notably those in the Levittown area. With the residential development of the farmlands of the county, what was once a thriving agricultural society turned into an increasingly residential and commercial area, with farmlands declining to almost nothing.

In the late 1950s, potato farmers were affected by the loss of Cuba as a selling partner. Previously, 5 to 8 percent of the Long Island crop had been sold to Cuba before Fidel Castro took power and the embargo was placed on trade between the United States and Cuba.

The ultimate fate of farming in Nassau County was the result of a combination of several factors. First, the end of World War II coincided with the increased use of the automobile and the idea of the suburbs. People were willing to settle farther away from the city, and Nassau County was in the sweet spot zone that was just far enough away to be a pleasant break from the bustle of the city yet not too far to make commuting an annoying nightmare. The young men who had been living at home before the war returned and were looking to settle down and start families, and the GI Bill gave them breaks and incentives that made homeownership possible for them. Demand for housing was high, not in the city but in Queens and Long Island. But there were certainly not enough existing homes to house them all. New homes would have to be built. The largest segment of "available" land was farms, and developers were able to snatch up farmland at prices that were attractive to both them and the farmers. At the same time, farm profits were in jeopardy anyway as supermarkets were opening everywhere, able to offer produce that was trucked in from elsewhere at often discounted prices. So, one by one, the farms of Nassau County and into western Suffolk were sold off and developed into tracts of residential homes. Levittown was probably the best-known example, but there were dozens of others like it. In 1947, developer William Levitt purchased about four thousand acres of potato farms in the Island Trees and Jerusalem area, just north of Wantagh, built hundreds of small single-family homes and called it Levittown.

By this time, the Mineola agricultural fair, mentioned previously, was also experiencing major changes; it was becoming less about agriculture and more about automobile races, rodeos, circuses, and daredevil stunts. A 1948 editorial in the *Hempstead Sentinel* explained, "Instead of dwindling on the vine, the Fair has become more robust with the passage of time. Now many industrial and commercial firms have joined the ranks of farmers and animal breeders as exhibitors, making the Fair larger in scope and more representative of the changing nature of Nassau County."

Winding Lane in Levittown, 1958. Just a decade earlier, the land was potato farms.

Youngs Farm in Old Brookville (seen here in 2021) is one of only three remaining farms in Nassau County.

By the 1950s, the fair had moved away from Mineola to the Roosevelt Raceway in Westbury before it relocated again to a more bucolic setting in Old Bethpage. It now has an old-timey nostalgic feel rather than its original purpose of being a place where farmers from all over Long Island could come together and show off their wares and learn of the latest farming tips and tricks.

Suffolk County remains an important agricultural region, providing fresh produce for Long Island and surrounding areas. Though farming is mostly lost in Nassau County, its heritage lives on; most of the county's villages and towns were founded and grew up on the strength of their farmers. No matter where we live, we must all remember that it is only thanks to the hard work of farmers that we have food on our tables every day.

Chapter 4

LOST FLORAL EMPIRE

Located in western Nassau County on the border with Queens, Floral Park is a small village with a big, fragrant past. Street names such as Carnation, Tulip, Verbena, Violet, Geranium, Primrose, Crocus, Gladiolus, Iris, and Pansy celebrate a long-lost heritage that is steeped in the thousands of colorful flowers of all kinds that used to grow there.

The village's blooming history began in 1874 with the arrival of a seventeen-year-old named John Lewis Childs from his native Maine to what was then known as the village of East Hinsdale. He got a job working for a local flower grower but was quickly able to rent a few acres of land, which was when he started his own nursery and florist business. Growth was slow at first, with sales from his first eight-page catalogue amounting to just fifty dollars. Determined, he worked hard and wound up buying the land he was renting. As his business grew, he continued to buy land, ending up owning much of what is now Floral Park and naming the streets accordingly. Childs was no ordinary seedman though. His business model did not just rely on locals and word of mouth. He not only sent out leaflets in the mail and began advertising his products in selected magazines, but in time, he also began publishing detailed catalogues and sending them to people across the country and around the world. He is credited as being the first person to start a mail-order seed business.

By 1901, he boasted of having 400,000 customers, and by 1915, that number was 500,000. By 1907, his company was sending out an astonishing 1 million catalogues a year. The village of Floral Park grew up around his

Above: The cover of the 1901 John Lewis Childs flower and seed catalogue.

Opposite: The order form from the 1901 John Lewis Childs catalogue.

Date.. *1901.*

John Lewis Childs, Floral Park, N. Y.

Dear Sir :—Enclosed please find $ ...., for which please send me the following

articles by (mail or express)...................... (Read General Instructions on page 1 of Catalogue).

Name, *(write plain,)*..

Post-Office, ...

County, ... **State,** ....

Name of Express Co. .... *Express Office.* ....

Quantity.	ARTICLES WANTED.	Price.
	We hope you will Subscribe for "The Mayflower." It will surely delight and help you.	

burgeoning business. It was incorporated in 1908, a direct result of the growth of his company and the jobs it attracted. The nursery catalogues were printed by the Mayflower Publishing Company in Floral Park (founded in 1892); Childs served as the president of that company, which in 1907 employed 60 people. He was also behind the founding of the *Schoolmate Monthly Magazine*, the official organ of the School Garden Association of America, aimed at kids and offering tips on gardening.

Childs's business model was a smart one; according to the 1901 catalogue, the company took the risk of accepting money by mail; sent seeds, bulbs, and plants free by mail; and guaranteed that the packages would reach their destination in good condition with every item true to name, and if anything was lost, they would remail it. All orders were filled as they were received so long as the stock was available, and the orders were packed carefully for safe transportation; they even offered discounts to some clubs.

By 1915, Childs's landholdings in Floral Park were about three hundred acres, including ten acres for his own residence (he also had another nine hundred growing acres known as Flowerfield in St. James, in Suffolk County). According to a biography, "some fifty or more young ladies are constantly booking and filling orders and a small army of boys and girls are needed to pack and prepare the seeds for shipment."

His catalogues were well illustrated with beautifully detailed drawings of flowers and fruits and featured extensive descriptions of the wares he was peddling. He was also forward thinking by placing a copyright notice on each of the elaborately drawn floral images in the catalogue to prevent others from stealing his pictures in their own catalogues. The entry on gladiolus from the 1901 catalogue read:

The Gladiolus is the most satisfactory, the most desirable and the most popular of all garden bulbs. Nothing else of the kind costs so little, and nothing else grows and blooms so readily for anybody and everybody in any soil or climate. It is, in fact, the most satisfactory garden flower, thriving and blooming, as it does, with the least care and attention, and makes a display which, for brilliancy and beauty of coloring, few bulbs can equal and none can surpass. The Gladiolus is to the flower garden what bread is to man, "the staff of life." Our collection is so large that many of the finest and highest priced sorts of European catalogues can be supplied by us by the tens of thousands and we can offer them at very low prices.

He offered a huge variety of flower seeds (at three cents a packet), including varieties that most of us had never (and still have never) heard of: *Centaurea Cyanus, Cherianmthuis, Escholotzias, Fenzxlia, Gypsophila Elegans, Maurandya, Nigella,* and *Hemophila.*

A wonder that was advertised in the 1901 Childs catalogue was the Apple Bismarck, which was a dwarf apple. The trees stood only approximately a foot high and would yield only a few apples but of a size much bigger than a normal apple. For thirty cents for one plant or fifty cents for two, someone could be the proud grower of an Apple Bismarck tree, whether in a pot or in the ground in the garden. It was billed as a unique plant that was a fine addition to any garden.

Childs's catalogues offered numerous varieties of popular flowers to attract even the most serious and ardent of horticulturists. For instance, in his 1901 catalogue, there were twenty-five kinds of sweet pea. He was also a writer, authoring such brief books as *An Illustrated Guide to Lily Culture* (1888). An aspiring politician, in 1894 he was elected to the New York State Senate. He also ran unsuccessfully twice for Congress as a Republican and was a strong supporter of fellow Long Islander Theodore Roosevelt.

He founded a magazine called *The Mayflower* (circulation 300,000), also printed by the Mayflower Publishing Company and devoted to "the cultivation of Flowers and Plants, Fruits, Vegetables, and to Gardening and Home Adornment in general." It was a smart business decision because it promoted interest in gardening among people most likely to order from

VOL. XVIII.   FLORAL PARK, N. Y., MARCH, 1902.   No. 3

✿ ✿ THE MAYFLOWER, ✿ ✿
PUBLISHED MONTHLY
AT FLORAL PARK, NEW YORK,
—BY—
The Mayflower Publishing Co.
JOHN LEWIS CHILDS, President.

Subscription Price, 25 Cents a year.
Foreign subscribers must send one shilling extra for postage.

THE MAYFLOWER is devoted to the cultivation of Flowers and Plants, Fruits, Vegetables, and to Gardening and Home Adornment in general.

Entered as Second Class Mail Matter at Floral Park P. O., N. Y.

Notice to Subscribers.

IF this notice is marked with a blue pencil, it shows that your yearly subscription has expired, and if you have not already renewed, no more copies will be sent until you do. Please renew promptly. Do not give street or number, or box number, in villages where it is not necessary to insure delivery of mails. Make addresses brief as possible.

Yearly subscriptions will begin immediately they are received, and the subscriber's name and address cast in stencil, and wrappers for 12 issues printed. This makes it impossible for us to change an address during the year's term. If subscribers change their address they must have their postmaster forward their copies to their new home.

The first page of the March 1902 issue of *The Mayflower*, a gardening magazine published by John Lewis Childs and printed at his complex in Floral Park.

his nursery. Because it was connected to his flower business, he could offer subscribers who spent the twenty-five cents for a year's subscription a special premium of a packet of flower seeds for an extra five cents. *The Mayflower* boasted a staff of over one hundred contributors representing every state. The July 1905 issue, for example, was entirely devoted to the verbena. He also ran *The Warbler*, a magazine devoted to birds.

Childs introduced something called the wonderberry or sunberry (also known as the garden huckleberry, a plant in the nightshade family), developed by the famous horticulturalist Luther Burbank. It became popular at the time because it was so easy to grow. One five-month-old plant Childs had bore 10,375 berries.

His vast fields of flowers could be seen by riders of the Long Island Rail Road, which itself was great advertising. A 1903 biography of Childs proclaimed that "the magnitude of the floral display is not equaled in America and probably not in the world." As of 1903, three catalogues a year were being issued, one January 1 (spring), one February 1 (specialties), and one September 1 (bulbs).

The home, lawn, and private conservatories of John Lewis Childs in Floral Park, circa 1905.

The publishing company was housed in a building that was 150 by 40 feet with seven presses, including a $16,000 rotary Web that could print a whopping eighty thousand copies of *The Mayflower* a day. There were also three trimmer machines, five stitching machines, a grinder, a steam pump, and an electrotyping operation. During peak months, Childs received eight to ten thousand letters a day from prospective customers; correspondence was handled by a staff of fifty. He also employed a full-time artist to photograph and sketch flowers and plants for use in his lavishly illustrated catalogues. He was so well known around the country that local newspapers everywhere featured stories on him; an editor in South Dakota wrote, "The greenhouses and flower gardens, the acres of roses, lilies and gladioli at Floral Park are worth a pilgrimage to see."

The business office was a four-story brick and iron building, which included a business office, an entire floor devoted to seeds and another floor for packing and mailing equipment. He basically built Floral Park, which included a seed and bulb house one hundred by forty feet and three stories high; five large greenhouses, two hundred by twenty-five feet; another nine houses; and then a further eight greenhouses for rare and fancy plants. In addition to those, there were another twenty buildings on the property that were used for the business, including a farmhouse with barns and stables, a steam lumber and planing mill, greenhouses, and a store. There were also brick cold sheds used to store plants in wintertime to fill orders to the southern parts of the country during Long Island winters. His business was so large that the government opened a post office in Floral Park to serve his needs. He received and shipped several tons of mail every day.

Along with his fondness for flowers, Childs was an avid ornithologist (i.e., he studied birds) and was arguably an expert given the fact that he had a collection of 1,130 birds and 1,030 species of eggs, some still preserved in their nests. He also collected butterflies, beetles, shells, and rocks, which were both personally collected by him and given to him by friends and customers from around the globe. He also collected books; he was said to have the finest private library in the world on North American natural history.

John Lewis Childs grew his beloved Floral Park into a thriving commercial enterprise, sharing what he loved with the people of Long Island and around the world. He worked hard all his adult life to create a beautiful, expansive floral paradise. Unfortunately, as with much that has happened on Long Island, circumstances changed quickly. Childs died in 1921, and in 1928, his widow and sons sold the business. The company went bankrupt and out of business just a few years later in 1931. The land was sold off and the buildings demolished, and today, the only trace of the old business is the fragrant street names such as Carnation, Tulip, Verbena, Violet, Geranium, Primrose, Crocus, Gladiolus, Iris, and Pansy. Hundreds of homes now sit on what used to be a massive floral empire.

Chapter 5

LOST GOLD COAST

Harbor Hill

The wealthy superstars of modern-day New York live in colossal mansions all along the South Fork, from the Hamptons to Montauk, on large flat strips of property overlooking the ocean. During the early twentieth century, though, the wealthy had their sights on an entirely different area of Long Island—the northern half of Nassau County and western Suffolk County. Known as the Gold Coast, this area was home to hundreds of impressive estates featuring large homes and landscaped formal gardens.

As mentioned in chapter 3, much of what would become the Gold Coast was for over a couple of hundred years quiet Quaker farms. The situation changed during the 1880s after the Meadowbrook Hunt and Polo Club opened on the Hempstead Plains, offering enticement to the super rich who wanted to either participate or spectate.

Between the 1890s and 1920s, large mansions sprung up by the dozens from Glen Cove to Brookville, from Roslyn to Huntington, from Westbury to Muttontown, designed by the country's best-known architects and situated on beautifully landscaped properties. Though spectacular in size and décor, the half-life of many of these great estates was only about thirty to fifty years from time of construction to time of demolition. There were various factors that contributed to their demise, including the financial hit of the Great Depression, the death of the original owners, the cost of upkeep, and fire or vandalism.

Clarence Mackay and his daughter at a wedding at the Church of the Advent in Westbury, 1915.

The largest example of a lost Gold Coast estate is the property owned by Clarence Mackay (1874–1938) in Roslyn. Mackay, financier and chairman of the board of the Postal Telegraph Cable Company, was also the heir to his father John Mackay's silver mining fortune. In 1898, he married Katherine Duer, a wealthy New York socialite.

The Mackays worked hard to find the right location for their country estate. They studied a map in a one-hundred-mile radius of New York City and visited hundreds of places over the course of two years, speaking with architects and landscape designers before settling on a 576-acre property at Harbor Hill, the highest hill in Nassau County (348 feet above sea level). Construction took place between 1899 and 1902, with four hundred men working on the completion of the house and grounds. The mansion was designed by the famous firm of McKim, Mead & White in the style of a French chateau and was an astonishing 238 feet wide by 110 feet deep. The main floor had 18-foot ceilings, and the second and third floors had ceilings of 15 feet. The main hall on the first floor was 40 feet wide by 80 feet long, off of which could be found many rooms, including salons, reception rooms, music rooms, a banquet hall, a dining room, a picture gallery, and breakfast room. In the full-sized basement were laundry rooms, storerooms, wine cellars, and a cold storage plant. Money was no object; one bathtub alone cost more than $17,000, made from a solid block of marble imported from Italy. Walls and ceilings from an old church in France were used with entire rooms shipped section by section from Normandy; there was also one of the world's finest collections of armor. Even the barn was fancy; it was tiled throughout and had Belgian brick floors and teakwood doors. The entire estate cost an estimated $8 million to complete.

The building of this enormous estate was news around the country. A 1906 Duluth, Minnesota newspaper article described what effort had to be made to create the estate:

> *To secure so large a block of land many small farms had to be wiped out and the farmhouses destroyed, a cemetery had to be removed and a street or two in the rural town of Roslyn had to be closed. To get the desired forest effect hundreds of old trees which stood in the wrong places had to be uprooted, while hundreds of others had to be planted full grown.*

So large was the property that the drive from the main gate to the mansion was a mile long, an uphill drive alongside flower gardens, lawns, and landscaped trees. A 1907 *Brooklyn Daily Eagle* article described one of the amazing features at Harbor Hill:

> *One of the principal features of detail at Harbor Hill is the lighting of the drive from the main lodge entrance to the house, there is no visible apparatus in the daytime, such as wires, poles, or lights, but at night a soft white light radiates out of the trees and bushes and brightens up the drive like day. This is arranged by an ingenious system of lamps in the trees, hidden in the foliage. The wires are all underground. Leaving the subway at the root of*

The Harbor Hill mansion was one of the largest homes ever built in the United States.

each tree selected for use, and well insulated to guard against fire, the wires run up the hidden sides of the trees and supply electricity for the bulbs that are buried away in the leaves. The effect at night is almost too beautiful for description. The trees and bushes seem to be aglow with soft white light as though they were some mysterious species of plant life that radiates light, of their own accord when the sun has gone to rest.

The estate had a total of seventy horses on the grounds. Ten stablemen were employed in the coach stable alone. The lawn was mowed once a week and the lawn directly in front of the house mowed three times a week.

The colossal Mackay mansion's landscaped grounds and gardens were by all accounts magnificent. A 1927 article referred to Clarence Mackay as the "country's most famous host." Guests who were entertained there included the Prince of Wales, for whom a $100,000 party was thrown in 1924, with 1,200 guests in attendance; F. Scott Fitzgerald; and Charles Lindbergh—just two days after his triumphant return to the United States after his transatlantic flight in 1927.

Despite all the money and luxury, the Mackays were not a family without controversy. In 1913, without warning, Mrs. Mackay packed her belongings and drove away from the Harbor Hill estate, never to return. At the same time, she filed paperwork to transfer the Harbor Hill estate entirely to her husband. She and Mackay divorced, and she married a surgeon named Dr. Joseph Blake, but not before being sued by the surgeon's then-wife, who accused her of causing the "alienation of affection" from her husband. Clarence Mackay remarried in 1931, only after his first wife had died. Mackay had a great relationship with his daughter Ellin until she married composer Irving Berlin, a match of which Mackay highly disapproved, and father and daughter stopped speaking.

The sheer size of the Mackay estate made its long-term upkeep impossible. Harbor Hill was abandoned in 1938 after Mackay's death because his son could not afford the upkeep. After the son inherited the property, he had to face the hard facts—there was no way for him to keep this enormous mansion and property. Despite all the splendor, the mansion's life span was less than fifty years. In 1943, the estate was taken over by the U.S. Army for use as a World War II military encampment. Wartime was also when the house was badly vandalized because police in the area were in short supply. It was demolished in 1947 over a six-week period, and many of the valuables inside were put up for auction, including fifty thousand cubic feet of granite slabs, one hundred tons of

The old gatehouse is one of the few remaining vestiges of Harbor Hill that stands today.

cast iron, piles of mirrors, carved wood panels, and tiles. The land was sold and subdivided in the late 1950s to become the Country Estates residential development, which includes hundreds of homes that have now been there longer than the Harbor Hill mansion itself stood.

All that is left of Harbor Hill today are a few small mementos of the once-gigantic estate. The most impressive remnant of the estate is the two-and-a-half-story former dairymen's cottage at 40 Elm Drive in East Hills (designed by Warren and Wetmore), which somehow survived all the destruction. The magnificent gatehouse still stands at the corner of Roslyn Road and Harbor Hill Road. Turn left onto Harbor Hill Road and then left again into Country Estates and you will come upon another remnant off Redwood Drive: an ancient-looking stone tower. Stanford White (the White in McKim, Mead & White architects) was hired to design an aesthetically pleasing structure in which to encase and disguise an ordinary-looking sixty-five-thousand-gallon water tank. Located as it was at a high point, the water distribution system relied on gravity to send water through a system of pipes to the mansion and other buildings on the property. White designed a quaint, sixty-five-foot-high thick-walled stone tower that looks like it belongs to a medieval European castle, in whose window at any moment a damsel in distress might appear calling for help.

Two twenty-six-foot-high horse statues on pedestals were installed at Harbor Hill in 1920. One statue was moved to the front lawn of Roslyn High School in the 1950s, and the other remained in place at what became Poplar Drive after the estate was developed, until it was installed at Gerry Park in 2013 (seen above).

After the mansion was demolished, the water tower remained because it could serve a function and provide water to residents of Roslyn, but the tank eventually wound up inactive. It is currently a spare tank, ready to be put into use in case it is needed, one of the last remnants of one of the most impressive estates ever built. One other remaining treasure from the lost estate are two horse statues that used to stand at the bottom of the west garden. One horse now stands in Gerry Pond Park in Roslyn, and the other is in the parking lot of Roslyn High School.

Most Long Island residents are probably not familiar with what once stood on the site of their current residence. This is also likely true for many of the hundreds of people who are currently living where the colossal Harbor Hill property stood. Once the most impressive estate in the country, Harbor Hill is now just another long-lost piece of Long Island history. It is still possible to enjoy the last few remains of this vanished estate, but from these precious remnants it is hard to truly grasp the opulent magnificence of the once illustrious Harbor Hill estate.

Chapter 6

LOST GOLD COAST

The Tiffany Estate

The name Tiffany is synonymous with high-quality, priceless decorative masterpieces, and rightly so. The Tiffany artistic dynasty began with Charles Lewis Tiffany (1812–1902), a businessman and the founder of New York City's Tiffany and Company, still in existence today on Fifth Avenue. Tiffany jewelry is known for its high quality and elegance, a standard within the jewelry world that is practically unmatched. He was a master at working in sterling silver, something Tiffany is still known for today.

When Charles Lewis Tiffany died, he left his son an impressive inheritance of $3 million. By this time, the younger Tiffany had achieved even more than his illustrious father. By the turn of the twentieth century, Louis Comfort Tiffany (1848–1933) was a world-famous master of glass art. His art was in magnificent private collections, in some of the finest museums, and decorating and illuminating public buildings such as churches. In his long and distinguished career, Louis Comfort Tiffany designed hundreds of intricate and elaborate stained-glass windows (some on a massive floor-to-ceiling scale) but also pieces of jewelry, vases, and lamps. He was also a noted painter and artist.

Though he owned a huge mansion on the Upper West Side of Manhattan and had other properties elsewhere, it was Tiffany's massive eighty-four-room Laurelton Hall on Long Island (started in 1902 and completed in 1904; it had twenty-six bathrooms!) that was the culmination of all his artistic endeavors, his signature way to fully express himself and display his creative

Louis Comfort Tiffany chose Long Island for his home.

genius. Located in the village of Laurel Hollow in the town of Oyster Bay, Laurelton Hall was Louis Comfort Tiffany's dream house.

In 1902, L.C. Tiffany purchased a four-story, one-hundred-room circa 1873 scenically situated resort hotel called Hotel Laurelton, which was just east of Oyster Bay village and near the Suffolk County border and Cold Spring Harbor. He felt this would be the ideal spot for his mansion. He also bought adjacent parcels of land to create his nearly six-hundred-acre country estate, demolishing the old hotel so he could build his $2 million (approximately $68 million in today's money) mansion on the site. Though other wealthy Gold Coast property owners hired renowned architects to design their palaces, Tiffany designed his house himself, planning the layout and the styles to the last detail, using an actual and relatively unknown architect only to draw up the official plans for the builder.

By all accounts, the house was like a museum, carefully curated by Tiffany himself, with both his works and other pieces from his collection (such as Native American baskets). The eight-level house with its copper roof was surrounded by beautiful terraced gardens, fountains, and pools. Tiffany was entranced by water, so he made sure to use it frequently as a point of visual attraction in his grounds. A visit to Laurelton Hall was an immersive and transformative experience into an exotic and lavish world of art and design; it was unlike any other mansion on Long Island.

Unlike most mansions of that time, the Tiffany home—Laurelton Hall— had no fireplaces because Louis Comfort Tiffany was afraid of a fire starting. So instead, he had a coal heating plant built on the property, which would burn coal and heat the enormous home. But for such a large building, a large heating plant would be required. And burning coal on that scale would require a fairly substantial smokestack, which could potentially be an eyesore for his neighbors.

However, in typical Tiffany style, he did not settle for either the ordinary or the ugly. Louis Comfort Tiffany's sixty-foot-high smokestack was a rather ornate affair, an attractive Moorish-style slender tower with a pointed top that looked a lot like a minaret but with beautiful blue stained-glass panels enshrined by pairs of columns just under its peak.

A front elevation of Laurelton Hall showing the belltower and projecting veranda, 1924.

Tiffany spent much time over the years at his estate, but he had bigger plans for it. In 1919, at the age of seventy, Tiffany created the Louis Comfort Tiffany Foundation to offer education to talented young artists trying to start their careers. He gifted his estate to the foundation (along with an endowment of $1 million) with the hopes it could serve as a live-in school and studio for artists, and over the next thirteen years, he provided support and advice to the many young people who benefited from his foundation.

Tiffany said at the time:

> *My intention is to provide a place where artists who have had elementary training, and who show real ability, can work in sympathetic and inspiring surroundings. There will, of course, be necessary rules which must be observed, but there will be no head master to provide cast iron methods of teaching to which all must conform. My hope is by stimulating love of beauty and imagination to give free play to development without the trammels, of schools or conventions.*

A view of the living room of Laurelton Hall with Tiffany stained-glass windows including *Feeding the Flamingoes*, *The Four Seasons*, and *The Bathers*.

After Louis Comfort Tiffany died in 1933, the foundation he had started continued to operate, until 1946, when it decided that maintaining the property was too expensive, so the trustees voted to sell the house's contents at auction—the very collection that Tiffany had worked so hard to assemble. There was a fear at the time that the house would "vanish under the hands of wreckers much as a fairy castle disintegrates at the wave of a wand" unless it was sold soon. The land and house itself were sold in 1949, but the impressive building then lay abandoned for several years. Tragically, the house burned down in 1957, probably due to vandals; unfortunately, it was never determined how the fire started. Although the smaller pieces and furniture had been sold, there was much that was lost in the way of integral architectural components and stained glass that Tiffany had designed for his house.

The largest piece that was saved from the ruins was a columnar screen that used to serve as the entrance to Laurelton Hall; that piece is now on display at the Metropolitan Museum of Art in Manhattan. In 2006–07, the Met held an exhibit called "Louis Comfort Tiffany and Laurelton Hall,"

The Laurelton Hall smokestack with its blue stained-glass decoration stands on private property, one of only a few remains of the great Tiffany estate after it burned down in the 1950s.

featuring some of the surviving furnishings and items that used to decorate the mansion. Many architectural and design elements (such as stained-glass windows) had been rescued from the burnt remains of the estate by Hugh McKean and his wife, Jeanette Genius McKean, founders of the Charles Hosmer Morse Museum of American Art in Winter Park, Florida, which houses many of these almost lost treasures. A thirteen-and-a-half-foot-high Vermont marble chimney breast in the dining room was the only interior architectural element to survive the 1957 fire.

Today, there are almost no remnants on the site of the glory that used to be the Tiffany estate. The land has since been subdivided and homes built on it. The most visible remnant of the once glorious Tiffany estate can only be spotted from a few remote vantage points. Ironically, the sixty-foot-high smokestack of the coal-burning heating plant down the hill and away from the main building, which existed precisely because there were no fireplaces in Laurelton Hall, was the only structure that was a survivor of the fire. A drive to the end of Laurel Hollow Road leads one to the Village Hall and a small beach. It is from here that the gorgeous smokestack, now in some lucky property owner's backyard, can be viewed. The blue Tiffany stained glass glimmers in the sunlight, a vivid reminder of the artistic mastermind who once lived on that spot and the magnificent estate of one of America's most beloved artists that tragically went up in flames.

Though some still stand today, most of the great Gold Coast mansions of the early twentieth century are long gone now. These lost Gold Coast estates were truly a magnificent part of Long Island's history. These days, most of us could only dream of living in a home as luxurious as the ones that used to occupy the Gold Coast.

While there are many reasons these estates were lost, a common theme was the exorbitant cost of keeping them running. The annual property tax on a Gold Coast estate today would be well over $500,000 per year. Add to that the cost of hiring multiple maintenance staff to maintain the lawns and landscape, clean the house, and take care of horses. To afford such a lavish lifestyle indefinitely requires an endless supply of money, something only the very richest of the rich might have. With real estate prices ever on the rise, it became much more cost-effective to sell these large properties and subdivide them into small estates or entire neighborhoods of homes. Often, there was a lag time between property sale and property development, resulting in these large mansions being abandoned, leaving them vulnerable to vandalism and arson. In some cases, a beautiful old mansion might have been saved if it could have been relocated, but these homes were simply too monumental in size. Once they were constructed, they were meant to stay where they were, unlike an average house that could be uprooted and moved elsewhere if needed.

Chapter 7

LOST TREE MOVING

Long Island homeowners often call arborists to get overgrown trees pruned or removed. The one thing they most likely don't need is having fully grown trees moved. But at the turn of the twentieth century, there was a huge demand for such tree-moving services, and the primary provider was one of Long Island's oldest businesses, Hicks Nurseries in Westbury.

Hicks has been serving the horticultural needs of Long Island since 1853, starting out as Isaac Hicks and Son, a small company supplying fruit trees to fellow Quakers living in the area. Located between Jericho Turnpike and the Northern State Parkway, present-day Hicks is a thriving garden center known for its spring flower show, its pumpkin-filled fall festival and its huge selection of Christmas trees and decorations. But today's Hicks, even though it is a Mecca for suburbanites looking to decorate their fifty-by-one-hundred-foot plots of land, is a far cry from what it used to be.

For several decades, the Westbury area remained largely the same—sleepy and quiet, populated by Quaker farmers. But by the early 1890s, Isaac Hicks and his son Edward noticed that local demographics were changing. Super wealthy folk from Manhattan and elsewhere off-island were coming to the Greater Westbury area to build palatial mansions. In the golden days of Long Island's Gold Coast (roughly the late 1890s through the 1920s), Hicks was the go-to nursery for the estate owners whose properties sometimes numbered in the hundreds of acres and whose formal gardens rivaled the best of the old English tradition across the ocean where many of their ancestors were from.

But it was not just abundant shrubs and flowers that these millionaire estate owners desired. They also wanted dozens of trees to decorate their magnificent properties—to line their long, majestic driveways or to ring their formal gardens. Not just seedlings, though. No, they did not want their homes to look newly built, with scrawny little sticks that were hardly impressive and would take years to create the desired impression; they wanted their properties to appear well established. Of course, most of these properties (some of which had belonged to Quakers) already had trees of some sort, but they were most likely not the desired type or in the right place.

Hicks was there for these new property owners, offering nearly full-grown trees of all types that would save up to twenty-five years of time, which for these magnates was important since many of them were already in their thirties or forties by the time they were building their homes. (Jay Phipps, for example, whose property would become Old Westbury Gardens, was thirty-two when the house was completed, and Oheka Castle in Huntington was completed when its owner, Otto Kahn, was fifty-two.) Who wanted to wait until they were elderly to enjoy the look and feel of a well-established garden?

Hicks started offering this tree planting service in the 1890s, by which time the nursery had been in business for almost forty years. It took foresight and time on the part of the Hicks family to be able to sell big trees (which had to be planted years ahead), so there was clearly some anticipation of such needs as they watched neighboring farmland start to be purchased by rich city folk. "For screens to shut out laundry yards, stable, or some objectionable feature, they are just the thing" (a problem very few Long Island homeowners might have today!) read one 1910 ad.

With their special tree-moving equipment (patented in 1898 by Edward Hicks) and plenty of manpower and horsepower (as of 1906, they had twelve tree movers on staff; that number would grow), Hicks was able to transport huge mature trees up to fifty feet tall and plant them successfully on properties all across the north shore of Long Island (and far beyond).

The patent application for this tree-moving equipment reads, in part:

> *Our invention relates to an improved apparatus for moving trees. Heretofore tree-moving devices of various sorts have been used, several of them being satisfactory for moving small trees, but none, so far as we are aware, (and we have had considerable experience with various forms of such apparatus,) are adapted to moving trees of any considerable size—say from ten to twenty-four inches in diameter or thereabout—because such prior apparatus*

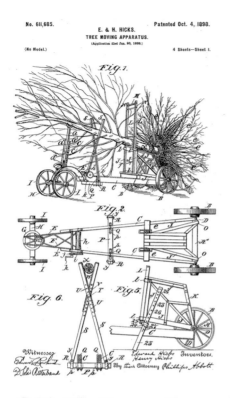

Left: Illustrations from Edward and Henry Hicks's 1898 patent application for tree-moving equipment.

Below: A 1907 advertisement touting the tree-moving services of Isaac Hicks & Son.

was not adapted to safely handle such large trees, and also because sufficient roots or earth-ball could not be transported with them, and, if not, the life or at least the thrift of the trees is doubtful.

The application goes on to describe the apparatus itself:

The rear ends of the perch are pivoted to the rear axle. Rigidly attached to this rear axle there is a cradle, which is adapted to tilt with it as an axis and to which the tree, which has previously been excavated, is lashed and by which it may be tilted over, suitable traction devices being provided, so that the cradle in its oscillatory movement will lift the roots and earth-ball free from the ground, lifting them into the air ten to fifteen or more feet, as the case may be. The front portion or top of the tree is supported upon suitable braces devices, which will be described hereinafter.

The trick was not so much just digging up large trees; a bunch of workers with shovels could do that. It was properly transporting such trees and planting them with well-protected and preserved root balls.

Hicks knew how to advertise to their wealthy target audience to continuously gain business. One 1907 advertisement read:

Think of having a shadeless, barren looking place today, and tomorrow wake up and find a tree 25 feet high sheltering one corner of your piazza or beautifying your grounds! It takes 25 years to grow such trees. Do you want to wait that long to grow yours? There is no risk in buying our big trees. We guarantee them to thrive. If they don't, your money back or a new tree.

A 1908 Hicks advertisement said:

Anyone can grow the smaller trees, but it took lots of enthusiasm, a good deal of capital and an unusual knowledge to produce these big trees.... When you stop to think of it, what a senseless thing it is to buy several small trees and plant them here and there on your grounds, and then have to be deprived of shade and their beauty for fifteen or twenty years when they grow up. Additionally, you spend your money for awnings, because you want immediate protection, then why not buy our large trees.

Their large tree offerings included Norway maples (as is true for many trees and ornamentals of the time, it is now considered a junk or weed tree but was then seen as desirable), sugar maples, silver maples and pin oaks. In 1909, a twenty-eight-foot-high silver maple that was sixteen years old cost thirty-five dollars, which was a lot of money for then; consider that the average baker made thirty cents per hour in 1909. It would take him fourteen and a half eight-hour days to earn enough to buy one of those large trees. But then again, such trees were not likely to be purchased by bakers or even bakery owners; they were intended for the super wealthy— for whom thirty-five dollars was a mere pittance. But still, for those who were more accustomed to spending thirty-five dollars on fine China than on a large tree, the ads had to appeal to their senses. According to a 1907 Hicks advertisement, "they are not a luxury, they are an investment." One 1908 advertisement was titled "About the Big Trees Like These That We Have Been Growing for You." In 1907, Hicks moved 175 evergreen trees between fifteen and thirty-seven feet high to the sixty-eight-acre Walter Oakman estate Oakdene in Roslyn in the space of nine months' time.

One of the most famous estates that Hicks served was the Clarence Mackay estate in Roslyn (see chapter 4). Isaac Hicks, the founder of the company, was actually born on the property long before it was owned by

A 1910 photograph shows the dozens of workers employed by Hicks.

Mackay. This estate, known as Harbor Hill, was composed of 576 acres with nine miles of private roads and one mile of water mains and one hundred servants. At the time, Harbor Hill was one of the largest mansions in the United States. It was demolished in 1947 and the property subdivided.

In 1908, Hicks & Son was hired and brought fifteen tree movers and laborers all the way to Washington, D.C., to excavate and move the historic "Crittenden memorial oak tree" while making way for the new General Ulysses Grant memorial. They also hired twelve local workers to assist in this effort. They moved the tree on timbers, greased bricks, and rollers along with a great ball of soil to ensure its survival.

During those days of the early twentieth century, Hicks had a selection of over one thousand of these large trees for estate managers to select from. How exactly did they accomplish moving these trees? According to one of their ads, "The roots are wrapped in damp moss, straw, and burlap, and tied in radiating bundles. The tops are trained with single leaders and flexible branches which tie in for shipping." They guaranteed their big trees and advertised that the trees could be shipped up to 1,500 miles.

In 1924, Hicks supplied trees to the Marshall Field estate; Field was heir to the department store fortune. The building, known as Caumsett Manor, is located in Lloyd Harbor in Suffolk County and was originally situated on two thousand acres. The mansion still stands today, now part of Caumsett State Historic Preserve.

Just how big was the Hicks property during these peak tree-moving years? So big that they could offer small evergreens for sale by the 100,000s, enough for "reforesting barren land." By 1928, the Hicks Nurseries property was two hundred acres in size, according to a Hicks catalogue, and "divided into blocks which are easily accessible by ten miles of good roads" set up so a visiting customer could drive around looking at all the plants and shrubs. "You can have almost as much quietness and beauty on an acre as on the place of fifty acres you envy." The property in 1939, after it was already reduced in size, was still seventy-five acres. In the years that followed, at least half of that land was sold off and developed for homes and the Drexel Avenue School. The current size of the property is about thirty acres.

With the vanishing of the great Gold Coast estates, Hicks Nurseries shifted gears and focused on its new primary clientele: the average homeowner who wanted to landscape and decorate their yard. No longer was there a need for mature trees to be planted on properties; most Long Island homes are now between 50 and 130 years old and already have fully grown trees. More commonly today, homeowners will purchase three- or four-foot-tall tree saplings at nurseries such as Hicks to plant themselves and nurture into fully grown trees over time. Some parents also want to plant trees when their children are born to watch them grow up as their children do. While today's technology would certainly allow mature tree moving to be done even more efficiently, there is simply no need for it anymore, deeming it a lost venture.

Chapter 8

LOST HOUSE MOVING

The mobile home is very much a product of the twentieth century and the invention of the automobile. Once cars were of a large enough size and had enough horsepower, towing around a home was made possible. This idea of the mobile home appealed to many Americans, with over four million of them currently in existence in the United States. Mobile homeowners enjoy the flexibility of having the ability to change locations as desired with ease and efficiency, whether remaining for long stretches of time in a trailer park or mobile home community or constantly on the go exploring the different areas of America.

Centuries ago, however, there were no such things as mobile homes; houses were built to be permanent, not to be moved. Transporting them was a rather complex and delicate operation, yet that did not stop people from doing it. In fact, between the seventeenth and twentieth centuries, moving entire buildings from one location to another, often miles away, was not uncommon at all!

Why would anyone want to move a house that was meant to be permanent? There are a few reasons. First, from the mid-1600s through the end of the nineteenth century, home building technology did not advance that greatly. Having a "newer" house was not an advantage, so saving an old one made sense and saved money. If you were living in 1850 in a house built in 1785, you'd want to try to keep it if possible, as it was sturdy and well made. In addition, there was no "real estate market" the way it exists today. If you had to move three towns over for business, you could not so easily just sell your house and buy a new one because houses were often passed down through the generations. Commuting even a few miles was much more of an ordeal in those days of horse and wagon, so that was not really an option. It was more efficient to buy a plot of land in the new town and have your existing house moved.

Long Island's history is filled with stories of old buildings that have been moved from their original locations. Two of the earliest known examples are in Cutchogue on the North Fork. One is the seventeenth-century Horton-Wickham-Landon House. Built in 1649 in Southold, it was disassembled board by board and moved several miles west to Cutchogue in 1661. Another is the Joshua Wells House, also known as Wells-Fleet-Goldsmith-Kendrick House or 1680 House, a historic one-and-a-half-story timber-framed residence that was built circa 1680 and extensively remodeled in 1815. The house has been moved twice and currently sits on a brick foundation constructed during its last move in 1857.

Originally the inn of Lieutenant Constant Booth, the two-and-a-half-story, nine-room Webb House in Orient (also on the North Fork) was built circa 1740 on Sterling Creek in the village of Sterling (later to become Greenport). In 1757, Colonel (and future president) George Washington

The Old House in Cutchogue was built in 1649 in Southold and moved to Cutchogue in 1660.

stopped at this inn en route from Boston to Virginia. The old building was moved in about 1810 to the North Road (present-day Route 48) and became the home of a man named Orange Webb. It was later purchased by George R. Latham, and in 1955, it was once again moved, to Orient, via barge. (At forty feet wide, it was too big to move along the road, so it had to make a half-mile journey across corn and potato fields to get to Sterling Creek, where it was loaded onto a barge.) It is now located in Poquatuck Park and is set up as an eighteenth-century tavern museum, displaying a collection of antiques and paintings.

The late eighteenth-century Nat Conklin House at 280 Deer Park Avenue in Babylon was moved from Main Street to its present location in 1871. In Westbury, the Finger family decided that their downtown home at the intersection of Post and Maple Avenues was in too busy of a location, so around 1915, Mr. Finger decided to have it moved north about a third of a mile away from the center of town, where it was quieter and more residential. The family went away on a vacation, and when they came back, the house had been moved, with everything inside still intact, to its new location on Wilson Avenue.

A three-story nineteenth-century Victorian house that was originally on the corner of Cathedral Avenue and Fifth Street in Garden City was moved in 1902 to 89 Fifth Street to make way for the Cathedral School of St. Mary. Owned by the Cathedral of the Incarnation of the Episcopal Diocese of Long Island, the building was given to the Garden City Historical Society under the condition that it be moved from the church property. It wound up being moved to municipal property in 1988, on Eleventh Street next to the Garden City Water Works.

How exactly were these moves accomplished? There were a few ways, but during the seventeenth and early eighteenth centuries, it would usually involve the use of horses or oxen to pull a building along a system of wooden rollers. Later eighteenth- and nineteenth-century house movers used screw jacks to push a house along greased steel beams that served as a track. These systems were not foolproof and sometimes resulted in structural damage to the building. More modern (nineteenth century and beyond) moves were accomplished by vertically lifting the structures and transporting them by truck.

Homes were not the only kinds of buildings that were moved. Quogue's first schoolhouse, built in 1822 and believed to be the oldest surviving schoolhouse in Suffolk County, was moved four times over the course of its existence, the last time being to its current spot on the Quogue Library property in 2019.

Meanwhile in Westbury, a new St. Brigid's Roman Catholic Church was built in 1894 on Post Avenue near the railroad station to replace a smaller, decades-old church. The parish was growing so fast, however, that by 1915, it was decided that an even larger church would be required to serve the influx of Italian immigrants who were coming to the area. On October 3, 1915, thousands watched as the cornerstone was placed for a new, larger structure. Granite blocks were brought in from New York City on the Long Island Rail Road, and the completed new church was dedicated in May 1916. During construction of the new building, the old 1894 building was painstakingly moved across Post Avenue to its present location in a process that took several months. It is said Mass was still celebrated in the old building as the church was in the process of being moved across Post Avenue. The old church was to serve as the first St. Brigid's School and now is known as St. Anthony's Hall.

The New Light Baptist Church was first organized in 1834 and was originally located at the present-day intersection of the Long Island Expressway and Glen Cove Road (Roslyn Heights). The wooden structure was moved to Westbury in 1867 to be more convenient to the many African Americans living in the neighborhood known as Grantville. It is today known as the African Methodist Episcopal (AME) Zion Church and still stands in Westbury.

The beautiful mansard-roofed Victorian building that houses the restaurant known as Westbury Manor (on the south side of Jericho Turnpike west of Carle Road) dates to the 1880s. It was originally owned by the Titus family and was first located on the north side of the turnpike and was bought in 1910 by the well-known local builder John R. Hill, who had it carefully dug out and moved to its present location. The eighteen-room house was occupied by Hill for many years but for a time during World War I rented to Mrs. Robert L. Bacon, the wife of congressman Robert L. Bacon. In 1946, it was reborn as a restaurant called Westbury Manor (also known for a time as Carl Hoppl's Westbury Manor; Carl Hoppl was a well-known baker). This is one of the largest known older examples of a Long Island building being moved.

In more recent years, most of the buildings being moved have been historic structures that were being saved from demolition and restored. One of the largest concentrated building moving efforts took place during the making of Old Bethpage Village in the 1960s. Nineteen historic buildings (as well as fifty smaller structures such as barns and outhouses) dating from between 1660 and 1875 from locations all across Long Island were moved

The building now known as Westbury Manor was moved across Jericho Turnpike in the early twentieth century.

These days, buildings are only moved for rescue purposes if they are of a historic nature. Seen here is one of the nineteenth-century structures at Old Bethpage Village, saved and moved from elsewhere on Long Island to this village recreation.

to this 165-acre former farm site to create a "village" (opened in 1970) that offers costumed inhabitants who give a living history appearance.

In 1973, a cow barn built in 1790 in Lloyd Harbor was moved to a new site at 434 Park Avenue in Huntington, next to the historic 1795 Kissam House. Moving and restoring the barn cost $25,000 and took fourteen months and many volunteers.

Today, the moving of houses and buildings other than historic ones that need to be saved has all but stopped. The main contributing factor to this is that technology has changed so rapidly in the last one hundred years or so that there is no viable reason to move a house that was built in, for instance, the 1950s to a more favorable location. Rather, it would be more reasonable and feasible to either build a new house in your desired location or simply purchase an existing home elsewhere. Additionally, the real estate market of today makes it relatively easy to sell a house in one location and find a new one elsewhere. If you traveled along the streets of Long Island, within the space of just a few blocks, you'd likely find several homes for sale. Lastly, with various travel and transportation advancements, commuting to work is much easier. It is not unheard of to have a job thirty or even sixty miles away from one's residence. While in the nineteenth century this commute would have been an untenable several hours long, these days it is manageable. While mobile homes are still around today, the moving of permanent houses is a lost Long Island art.

Chapter 9

LOST POLO ISLAND

The Gold Coast of Long Island was home to hundreds of wealthy families, many of whom were fans of one of the "richest," most exotic, and most action-packed of sports: polo. Polo is a game that is played between two teams on horseback. Each team uses mallets with long and flexible handles to move the ball down the field and in between the goal posts. Located just to the south of the hilly Gold Coast, the Hempstead Plains offered two of the requisite things for playing polo: lots of available open space and flat, unencumbered land. And of course, the third requirement was horses, of which there were plenty in the area back at the turn of the twentieth century. A polo field is 300 yards by 160 yards—the size of nine football fields!

Though it originated in Asia centuries ago, the modern form of polo was developed in India. The first European polo club opened in Assam, India, in 1859. The game of polo is played in eight periods of six minutes each, called chukkas. There are only four players per team; each one rides a horse (or "pony," hence the term "polo pony"). The players swing fifty-two-inch-long wooden mallets trying to hit a small ball (only three inches in diameter) across the field and into the opposite team's goal while at the same time defending their own goal. They usually switch horses after every chukka, as the game can get quite intense. Polo involves great manual dexterity and coordination, as well as the ability to control your horse quite precisely. The game of polo has contributed to American style with the ubiquitous "polo shirt" and a fragrance called Polo by Ralph Lauren. There are now also U.S.

Polo Assn. clothing stores, which are sanctioned by the governing body for polo in the United States.

Long Island's Meadowbrook Polo Club (originally Meadow Brook) had its origins in Mineola in the 1870s and was incorporated in 1881 in Westbury. Among its founders were Thomas Hitchcock, Oliver W. Bird, August Belmont, and Benjamin Nicoll. The first polo field in the area was built in 1884. The club's longtime location was near what is now the intersection of Stewart and Merrick Avenues. This club was also under the same umbrella as the Meadowbrook Hunt Club, which counted among its participants Theodore Roosevelt. The playing field, stands, and clubhouse were directly adjacent to Roosevelt Flying Field (and later Roosevelt Raceway—a harness racetrack that closed in 1988—when the eastern half of the airfield was sold). It was also across the street from the Salisbury Links golf club, founded by Boston Red Sox owner Joseph Lannin in Garden City a few years earlier but relocated to what would become the site of Eisenhower Park in 1917. Meadowbrook even had its own Long Island Rail Road station directly adjacent to the club (which continued to serve Roosevelt Raceway after the demise of the Meadowbrook Club but was discontinued in 1961).

Some of the greatest polo players of the era bought estates in the area. Thomas Hitchcock Sr. bought an old Quaker estate in Old Westbury just north of Jericho Turnpike that was a straight shot to the club down what is now Post/Merrick Avenue. His son Thomas Hitchcock Jr. was also a great polo player, actually surpassing his father; he was considered the Babe Ruth of polo. A sporting magazine wrote of Hitchcock Jr. in 1921:

> *Young Hitchcock swung a polo stick at an extraordinarily early age. So much you will realise when I state that when he was sixteen years old he was taking part in games with players of high handicap....Mid-way through the season of 1920 it was obvious that he was fulfilling his early promise in the game. He helped Meadowbrook to win the Senior Championship of America.*

Another article from 1921 said, "His experiences in aviation during the war, his capture by the enemy, and his sensational escape over the Swiss frontier—the only man to take that route—should give him poise beyond his years, and he may be depended upon to play a scintillant, brilliant game." *Time* magazine in 1927 wrote that Hitchcock Jr. was "sometimes described as 'the most brilliant polo player in the world.'" He was a "10-goaler," which meant he had a handicap of 10, which is the highest possible rating a polo

An international polo match at the Meadowbrook Club in June 1914.

player can have, a feat he achieved at age twenty-two, the youngest ever to have done that at the time. All in all, there have only been a handful of American 10-goalers in the history of the sport. Tom Buchanan in F. Scott Fitzgerald's *The Great Gatsby* was modeled after Thomas Hitchcock Jr.

Another well-known Meadowbrook player, Devereux Milburn (1881–1942), was married at the Church of the Advent on Jericho Turnpike in Westbury and was a lawyer when he was not at the Meadowbrook Club playing important matches. He played on every U.S. polo team between 1909 and 1927. He was one of the players who brought back the international polo trophy to the United States in 1909 after England had it for twenty-three years. It was written of him in 1921: "His principal asset is a wonderful command of the ball, and his ability to score backhand strokes from all kinds of apparently impractical angles has been generally attributed to luck, when, in reality, it is nothing of the kind but merely a thoroughly developed stroke."

Another famous old-time polo player was none other than Michael Grace Phipps (1910–1973), son of Jay Phipps, who was also a polo player and the founder and owner of Westbury House and the Gold Coast estate that would become today's Old Westbury Gardens.

Match attendees in the 1910s got to witness history in the making as some of the early airplane flights passed overhead. In 1911, aviator St. Croix Johnstone flew two thousand feet overhead, circling the polo field several times on the course of a thirteen-mile flight that had begun four

The Meadowbrook clubhouse building, circ 1910–15.

Star polo player Foxhall Keane at the Meadowbrook Club in 1914. Keene was an Olympic Gold medalist in the 1900 Olympics.

miles away in Garden City. Two days later, Johnstone flew over the polo field and dropped a small American flag from his plane as a symbol of good luck for the American team that was playing a match that day against another country.

In 1900, a mixed U.S. and Great Britain team won the gold medal at the summer Olympics. In 1920, the United States team won a bronze medal at the Olympics, and in 1924, the U.S. team won a silver medal. Thomas Hitchcock Jr. was a member of the 1924 team.

So popular was polo that huge crowds descended on the Meadowbrook Club for key matches, especially the annual Open events and the Westchester Cup matches between the United States and England. In 1936, a record crowd of thirty-eight thousand people attended a match at the field. Traffic approaching the field was backed up for hours such that by the time everyone was parked, the game had already begun.

The club would sometimes hold something called Camera Day, which was a chance for amateur photographers to go down to the polo field and take pictures of players in action during the game but also have the players stage action shots for them.

The polo matches were also a lesson in fashion and style, with outfits and accessories making the newspapers. A 1930 advertisement for the famous Philadelphia department store Wanamaker noted that knitted suits "were the rule of the day at the Meadowbrook Polo Games," as well as hats "moulded and draped to your head." "The smartest sports costumes were fashionably replete with hats made of the suit fabric."

World War II changed life on Long Island, and with the end of the war, some of the popular prewar activities and places faded away as tastes and life itself changed. Polo was one of those casualties, though it did make a bit of a resurgence. By 1953, the area itself was changing and becoming more industrial instead of the semi-rural playground it had previously been. Prior to 1953, when the club was in full operation, all its property holdings consisted of 326 acres. In 1953, however, under threat of condemnation because the state wanted to build a highway partly on its property, it sold 160 acres to the Jones Beach State Parkway Authority for construction of the Meadowbrook State Parkway, for $960,000 ($10.8 million today). The board of directors of the Meadowbrook Club then decided to move the club elsewhere and sell the remaining pieces of the old site. Later in that year, Meadowbrook sold 42 acres to the Old Country Trotting Association for $650,000 for use as part of Roosevelt Raceway. The rest of the parcels were soon sold as well, but the storied polo club's famous site came to a controversial end as the club was involved in a 1958 lawsuit over zoning issues (*United States v. Meadow Brook Club*).

For decades, the estate of the famous Hitchcock polo family in Old Westbury was still in existence, even though Thomas Hitchcock Sr. died in 1941 and his son died tragically soon after when the plane he was testing crashed during World War II in 1944. The property stayed in the family for some years but then went to other owners. In the 1990s, the property was seized by the federal government after a government sting operation. It was purchased by the Diocese of Rockville Centre, which after years of legal wrangling converted the old polo estate into the Queen of Peace Cemetery. For many years, the old stables where Hitchcock kept his horses were still largely intact, and the outline of Hitchcock's old full-sized racetrack could be easily spotted in aerial views of the property.

Meanwhile, the Meadowbrook Club relocated first to Jericho, but that field was sold for development in 1968, and the club then moved to Whitney Lane in Old Westbury, where it currently resides and has experienced a resurgence in popularity. The sport of polo is still alive and well on Long Island and therefore is not itself lost, but the famed old polo field site of numerous international tournaments is long gone.

Chapter 10

LOST AUTO RACING

Imagine automobile races taking place on local roads such as Jericho Turnpike and Hempstead Turnpike rather than a closed track. It seems impossible to conceive of this notion, yet this was exactly what happened on Long Island for several years in the early twentieth century.

Some of the earliest milestones in automotive history took place on Long Island, all the way back when cars were still an overwhelming rarity on roads that were largely populated by horse and carriage. The first ever car-train crash took place on Long Island in 1901. In 1903, racing trials were held on Long Island for the Gordon Bennett Cup Race in Ireland. The racecourse ran a length of six miles from Westbury south to Merrick.

The first international road race, held on Long Island in October 1904, was the idea of one of the country's biggest automobile enthusiasts (and one of the first Americans to import European cars to the United States), William Kissam Vanderbilt II. The heir to the Vanderbilt fortune and descendant of Cornelius Vanderbilt, he was a car owner by 1900, long before most Americans. The racing event he created was to be called the Vanderbilt Cup Race, and its start/finish line was in Westbury. Vanderbilt himself donated the prize, an engraved sterling silver cup. The total length of the racecourse was about 285 miles (a total of ten laps around the course, consisting entirely of existing local roads).

The racecourse was a loop that began and ended at Westbury, where a grandstand capable of holding one thousand people was constructed. The racecourse passed through Westbury, Jericho, Hicksville, Bethpage,

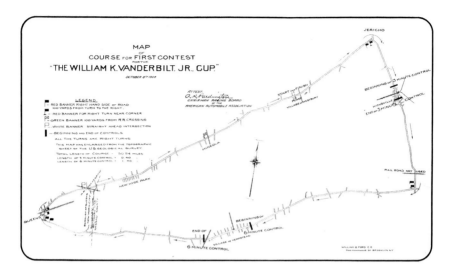

The 1904 racecourse of the Vanderbilt Cup Race. Drivers passed through Westbury, Jericho, Hicksville, Hempstead, and New Hyde Park.

Hempstead, and then into Queens, through Floral Park, to Mineola and then back to the finish line in Westbury. Much of the race was along Jericho Turnpike and Hempstead Turnpike, which in those days were dusty and unpaved. Some area residents were opposed to having cars zoom by on their local roads and protested to the race's board of supervisors, but to no avail. According to the *New York Herald* of September 27, 1904: "Agents of the American Automobile Association have covered the dead walls, fences and every available space on the Nassau County roads with placards warning the residents against running into danger" during the Vanderbilt Cup Race. These notices told people to take safety precautions, warning them "against allowing domestic animals or fowls to be at large during the race and are further cautioned against allowing children, unattended, to make use of these highways."

The entry fee was a steep $300 (in today's money, almost enough for a down payment on a house), half of which was a deposit that was returned if the car started the race. Working-class people made an average annual salary of $490, so to say this was a luxury is an understatement. Race preparations were extensive (including building the grandstand on Jericho Turnpike in Westbury), and local newspapers had stories about the upcoming race on an almost daily basis for weeks. Days before the race, ninety thousand gallons of crude oil mixed with water was spread across the course to provide traction for the racecars. This caused distress among homeowners, as the sticky black stuff was tracked into their houses and onto expensive carpets. The stench of the oil was also a complaint, as was the fact that horses' legs were getting splattered.

The race started at 6:00 a.m., so spectators had to arrive quite early in the morning. Some adventurous spectators even ventured out along the racecourse and crossed the road between passing racecars, despite warnings to the contrary. The winner of the 1904 race was George Heath, an American-born British citizen living in France. He was driving car number 7, a French-made four-cylinder Panhard & Levassor with a seventy-five-horsepower engine. Heath finished the course in a time of five hours, twenty-six minutes, forty-five seconds, averaging a little more than fifty-two miles per hour over the entire race. It does not seem very fast at all by today's standards, but to the average person in 1904, used to a horse and carriage traveling a few miles an hour, it was madness. Second place went to A. Clement Jr., driving a ninety-horsepower Clement Bayard, less than two minutes behind the leader's pace.

The race should have continued, but after the second car came across the finish line, the crowd began to leave, blocking the racecourse and ignoring Vanderbilt's pleas to clear the way. The race had to be stopped. It was a success overall, except for a racer who was injured when his car overturned and his mechanic, who was killed. Still, the *New York Times* proclaimed, "The contest was not as exciting as a horse race.…For long stretches of time there was nothing to be seen" but went on to say "and yet it was an impressive sight.…These ugly-looking mechanical demons whizzed by so fast that often they were nothing but a streak."

The Vanderbilt Cup Race was held again the next year, and the entry fee was raised to $500, with no refund. The 1905 racecourse was very different. Jericho Turnpike was the southernmost part of the course; it passed through Albertson, Roslyn, Greenvale, Brookville, and East Norwich. The average speed of the 1905 winner was more than sixty miles per hour, with at least one driver hitting almost ninety miles an hour on the straightaway. George Heath, the 1904 winner, came in second place. The crowds were large; in 1905, 100,000 people watched the race. Hotels in the area were booked up weeks in advance, and farmers and homeowners along the racecourse took advantage of the desperation of the race spectators, charging up to $50 for lodgings (a lot for a time when a men's suit could be had for about $5). As a newspaper of the time said, these were "figures which would make the average Broadway hotel resemble a Salvation Army lodging house."

The earliest documented use of a checkered flag to signal the end of an auto race was in the 1906 Vanderbilt Cup Race, which went through Lakeville, Searingtown, Manhasset, Roslyn, Brookville, East Norwich, Jericho, Westbury, and Mineola. In this same race, a spectator was killed by a racecar. Tearing up the racecourse at a pace of sixty-one miles per hour was the Frenchman Louis Wagner, who drove his one-hundred-horsepower Darracq car to victory. Lancia, in an Italian Fiat, was second, beaten by little more than three minutes. Duray of France was third in a De Dietrich, only sixteen seconds behind the second man. One Manhasset resident told a newspaper reporter:

> *I have seen all kinds of sport in my time. I like contests of every sort, although there is a good deal of Long Island Quaker blood in my veins. Still I enjoy the Vanderbilt cup race more than any event that I ever saw. Why, it was the awakening of this old village. There never was as much activity in this village in its history as there was last year. We are feeling the good effects yet. The people of this Village will be willing to make any reasonable sacrifice to have the race again.*

However, after the 1906 race, the Racing Board of the American Automobile Association held a meeting in the Garden City Hotel and decided that no more races should be held under the auspices of the association on that course. The board chairman said this was because it was impossible to keep the crowds of spectators in check and to avoid accidents. He said that in the future, if similar contests should be decided upon, they would be held at some place farther down the island.

There was no 1907 race, and in 1908, the race ran through Westbury, Jericho, Woodbury, Bethpage, and Central Park (what is now Levittown). Vanderbilt had by this time begun to build his Motor Parkway, the country's first modern highway, with the dual purpose of being a racecourse and a toll highway; 9 of the 23.46 miles of the course were run along the Motor Parkway. In 1909 and 1910, the race was run along the same course, a much shorter circuit of 12.64 miles, of which 5.15 were run along the Motor Parkway.

The headlines about the 1910 race, which was viewed by 250,000 spectators along its twelve-mile course, told a gruesome story:

HARRY GRANT IN ALCO CAR WON VANDERBILT CUP RACE
Dead or Wounded Marked Nearly Every Mile of the Course.

Scene from the 1908 Vanderbilt Cup Race showing driver Salzman near the grandstand.

NEW RECORD FOR AMERICA
Winner's Time an Average of 65 2-5 Miles an Hour—Harold Stone
Badly Injured and Expected to Die—Mechanicians Charles Miller and
Matthew R. Bacon Killed—Race Was Thrilling from a Sporting Point
of View—Judged by its Cost in Dead and Maimed, however, it Was a
Revolting Spectacle.

Aside from driver and mechanic casualties, several spectators were also badly injured. That was the last time the race was held on Long Island's roads; the 1911 race was moved to Georgia, and in 1912, it was held in Wisconsin. But that was not the end of auto racing on Long Island under the Vanderbilt name. In 1936, a new closed racetrack was begun in Westbury, on the site of Roosevelt Field number 1 (the eastern portion of the airport), the one from which Lindbergh had lifted off the ground and adjacent to the Meadowbrook Club. Present at the June 12, 1936 dedication ceremony for the new racetrack was Kermit Roosevelt, son of Theodore Roosevelt and brother of Quentin Roosevelt (who had died in World War I), after whom Roosevelt Field was named.

This new Roosevelt Raceway brought the return of the Vanderbilt Cup (now called the George Vanderbilt Cup; George was the nephew of William

Harry Grant winning the 1910 Vanderbilt Cup Race. It would be the last Vanderbilt Cup Race on Long Island until it returned to a closed track in Westbury in 1936.

K. Vanderbilt Jr.) to Long Island. The course was built in just eighty-three days, and the track was tested in September 1936, when thousands of cars, both racers and leisure drivers, ran the course for the first time.

There were forty-five entrants into the first official George Vanderbilt Cup Race on October 12, 1936. The field included such well-known racers of the time as Wild Bill Cummings and Billy Winn. A crowd of more than fifty thousand witnessed the three-hundred-mile race from the multi-tiered grandstand. The course included a 3,775-foot-long straightaway that allowed cars to reach speeds upward of 150 miles per hour. Only thirty of the forty-five racers finished the race. The winner of the contest was Tazio Nuvolari, a forty-year-old Italian driving a twelve-cylinder Alfa Romeo for a time of four hours, thirty-two minutes, forty-four seconds, at an average speed of nearly 66 miles per hour, negotiating around a total of 1,200 hairpin turns! Nuvolari received an engraved cup as well as a $20,000 prize, beating out the second-place finisher, Jean Pierre Wimille of France, by eleven minutes and fifty-seven seconds. The first American to finish the race was Mauri Rose of Ohio, who came in sixth place.

After the 1936 race, the course was modified to increase the average speed by removing many of the twists and turns. It evidently worked, because a

German racer doing a test run in June 1937 hit a record 158 miles per hour on the course. A crowd of seventy-five thousand people witnessed the 1937 George Vanderbilt Cup. The *New York Times* hailed the race beforehand as the "greatest auto race in history," but Americans were very disappointed when the German racer Bernd Rosemeyer won the contest, with an average speed of eighty-two miles per hour.

In August 1939, a three-hundred-lap midget car race (the first national championship) was held at Roosevelt Raceway, but that pretty much marked the end of the Raceway's automotive history for a while. The next and last Vanderbilt Cup Race at Roosevelt Raceway would not be held until 1960, when it was sponsored by another member of the Vanderbilt family, Cornelius Vanderbilt IV, nephew of William K. Vanderbilt, who had died in 1944. An American racer named Harry Carter won. There was also a special exhibition of old racecars, including "Old 16," the Locomobile that was the first American car to win a Vanderbilt Cup Race, in 1908. The 1960 contest would be the last of the Vanderbilt Cup Races.

Auto racing does still happen on Long Island, notably at the Riverhead Raceway, which began operation in 1951 and is the only NASCAR track in the New York metro area. The glory days of the illustrious Vanderbilt Cup Races, however, are long gone.

Chapter 11

LOST AVIATION PIONEERS

For almost forty years, Long Island was home to the nation's premier airport. Roosevelt Field was one of the nation's best known and most historic airports in America for many reasons, but it was a single event that propelled it into the national memory forever. Charles Lindbergh's landmark solo flight across the Atlantic Ocean in May 1927 made headlines in newspapers around the globe and brought the spotlight to Roosevelt Field. When his plane the *Spirit of St. Louis* landed in France thirty-three and a half hours later, he became the first person ever to fly solo nonstop across the ocean. Though this was an amazing moment in aviation, by that time, aviators had been making history on Long Island for nearly twenty years already, and it was through their efforts that Lindbergh's flight was made possible.

It all started with an upstate New York native and aviation pioneer named Glenn A. Curtiss, who was working out of a town called Hammondsport on Keuka Lake (one of the Finger Lakes). In 1908, he won the first leg of the Scientific American trophy for a flight of at least one kilometer. Soon after, Curtiss was sponsored by the New York Aeronautical Society, which paid him to build a plane to promote aviation for them. He initially flew the *Golden Flyer*, aka *Gold Bug*, from the society's field in the Bronx in June 1909, becoming the first person to fly a plane in New York City. The society had intended him to use their field as his base of operations, but Curtiss told them it was not big enough and so they set about looking for a better spot for a flying field.

Glenn Curtiss's airplane on the ground in Mineola in 1909.

Working together, they chose the Hempstead Plains on Long Island. It was the largest prairie east of the Mississippi River and was also largely undeveloped, so it offered thousands of acres of flat, unobstructed fields for planes to take off and land. The New York Aeronautical Society promptly leased some land in Mineola just east of Washington Avenue and just south of Old Country Road (adjacent to the Mineola Fair) from the Garden City Company. After a few days of preparations, this piece of land became Long Island's first flying field.

On July 13, 1909, Glenn Curtiss flew his plane for 1.5 miles in three minutes. It was the first successful airplane flight on Long Island. On the next day, he flew 5 miles; on the fifteenth, he flew 6 miles; and on the sixteenth, he managed to fly 15 miles. Having previously won the first leg, Curtiss was aiming for the second leg of the Scientific American trophy, a prize that was being offered to the first aviator to fly at least 25 kilometers (15.5 miles). On July 17, Curtiss felt he was ready to try for the prize, along an aerial course of 1.33 miles.

According to Curtiss himself in *The Curtiss Aviation Book* (1912):

> *It was a memorable day for the residents of that particular section of Long Island, who had never seen a flying machine prior to my brief trial flights*

there a few days before. They turned out in large numbers, even at that early hour, and there was a big delegation of newspapermen from the New York dailies on hand. Flying was such a novelty at that time that nine-tenths of the people who came to watch the preparations were skeptical while others declared that "that thing won't fly, so what's the use of waiting 'round." There was much excitement, therefore, when, at a quarter after five o'clock, on the morning of July 17, I made my first [official] flight. This was for the Cortlandt Field Bishop prize of two hundred and fifty dollars, offered by the Aero Club of America to the first four persons who should fly one kilometer. It took just two and a half minutes to win this prize and immediately afterward I started for the Scientific American trophy.

He flew nineteen laps around his course for a total distance of twenty-five miles, continuing on even after he'd passed the twenty-five-kilometer mark, and easily won the prize.

With that, aviation on Long Island was off to a powerful start. By 1910, another flying field had opened farther west, on Nassau Boulevard in a neighborhood called Garden City Estates. This 350-acre aerodrome, as it was called, became the new hot spot for flying on the island, with about twenty hangars in operation by 1911. Among the aviators who used this field was T.O.M. "Tommy" Sopwith, an English flyer and airplane designer whose Sopwith Camel was not only an important World War I plane but also gained later fame as the plane that the comic strip hero Snoopy used as he flew imaginary battle missions. Sopwith was one of the first to take passengers in the air. An article in *Country Living in America* said, "Passenger carrying has been demonstrated as feasible—and especially thrilling and enjoyable for the passenger—by Mr. T.O.M. Sopwith at the aerodrome. Many men and women have taken advantage of this opportunity to fly." His early guests included at least three women, who were among the first women in the country to fly in an airplane. In July 1911 at Nassau Boulevard, Sopwith set a new precision landing record, coming down only one foot, five and a half inches from the designated spot.

From October 22 to 30, 1910, the first international air meet in the country was held at Belmont Park. This major event attracted more than thirty aviators, who came both to watch and participate in the events. Wilbur and Orville Wright themselves showed up to the meet. A total of $70,000 in prize money was offered to the competitors. Most notably, aviators competed for a $10,000 prize in a race to the Statue of Liberty and back, which was won by English aviation pioneer Claude Grahame-White. On October 25,

The Belmont Park Aviation Meet in 1910 brought many of the world's best aviators together in one place for contests and stunt performances.

Ralph Johnstone broke the altitude record by ascending to a height of 7,303 feet, through a snowstorm no less!

Meanwhile, Alfred Moisant and partners had started an aviation school out of the Nassau Boulevard Aerodrome, but in December 1910, they leased a large tract of Hempstead Plains land farther east near Westbury. The school transferred over to the new field even as they were still building all their planned infrastructure, which was to include a clubhouse and grandstand for spectators. The school's earliest instructors were all French aviators. By early May 1911, there were forty-two students enrolled in the flying school. The Moisant School is where the first woman pilot in the country learned to fly—Harriet Quimby, an editor for *Leslie's Weekly* newspaper in Manhattan. Two other prominent flying schools of the time did not accept women students, so the Moisant School was ahead of its time. After two weeks of lessons, Quimby made her first flight on May 11, 1911. In August 1911, Quimby received her license from the Aero Club of America, which at the time was the organization that bestowed official flying licenses. At that time, there were only thirty-nine licensed pilots in the entire country, and Quimby was for a brief while the only woman in the world licensed to fly a plane. That same year, Quimby set a world record for precision landing, coming down seven feet, nine inches from the marked spot. Sadly, Quimby was killed in a plane crash in Massachusetts in 1912.

According to one of its advertisements in a trade magazine at the time, the Moisant School had a 1,200-acre field "level as a billiard table" for exclusive use of Moisant pupils. "No Trees. No Hills. No Electric Wires. Concrete Fireproof Hangars." The concrete hangars with iron-roll doors were supposedly the first in the world. The word "fireproof" was not just a slogan. A couple of years after the hangars were built, a fire ravaged a nearby hangar, but the Moisant hangars were safe.

In July 1911, Chicago aviator St. Croix Johnstone broke the American flight endurance record flying out of the Mineola field in a Moisant monoplane. He stayed aloft for four hours, one minute and fifty-three and three-quarter seconds, circling the aviation field of about five miles a total of thirty-nine times at about sixty miles per hour. He would have gone longer on his fifty gallons of gasoline if not for engine trouble that forced him to land, but he still broke the previous endurance record by twenty-two minutes. The first aviators were often called "bird men," and those who had flown before 1917 were later known as "early birds."

In September 1911, the International Aviation Tournament was held at the Nassau Boulevard Aerodrome in Garden City. Competitors from all over the country gathered to perform flying acrobatics and win prizes. There was a speed contest for monoplanes, and Claude Grahame-White won the prize of $600, flying ten miles at an average speed of sixty-one and a half miles an hour. Matilda Moisant went up to an altitude of 1,414 feet, which at the time was an astounding height. There was a bomb dropping contest, and the winner managed to drop their missile just five feet and nine inches from the bullseye.

The most exciting event of the air meet was dreamed up by the postmaster of the United States, Frank Hitchcock, who had the idea that mail could be delivered long distances using airplanes rather than the much slower method of ground transportation. Aviator Earle Ovington was chosen to be the first airmail pilot, and a postal tent was set up on the Nassau Boulevard fairgrounds for attendees to write postcards and be part of this historic flight. There were twenty mailboxes on site, which were emptied and the contents brought to the tent where the mail was canceled. On September 23, 1911, after being officially sworn in as the Postal Service's first airmail carrier, pilot Ovington took off in a Bleriot XI airplane with a sack of mail. Because there was so much mail (781 letters, 6,165 postcards and 55 pieces of printed

Earl Ovington piloted the first airmail flight in the country during the International Aviation Tournament at the Nassau Boulevard Aerodrome on September 26, 1911. Ovington is seated in his Bleriot airplane; also in the photo are Frank Harris Hitchcock, postmaster general; and Edward M. Morgan, postmaster of New York.

matter), it was more than one aviator could handle, and the mail was split into two bags of sixteen pounds and fourteen pounds. Tommy Sopwith volunteered to carry the second bag, and the men took off. When the aviators reached Mineola, where the postmaster of Brooklyn and a postal inspector were waiting in a field, the aviators dropped the mail sacks. The historic mail they carried was postmarked "Aeroplane Station No. 1 Sept. 23, 1911 p.m. Garden City Estates, N.Y." and had a special stamp that read "AERIAL SPECIAL DESPATCH."

While Ovington was airborne that day, he penned the first letter ever written in an airplane. He brought with him a blank sheet of paper signed by three newspaper reporters, so nobody could accuse him of bringing an already-written letter with him into the plane. With the paper on his knee and the pen in one hand, while steering with the other hand, Ovington wrote the following to Timothy Woodruff, president of the Aero Club and founder of the Nassau Boulevard Aerodrome: "Congratulations on the success of America's most successful aviation meet. Sincerely yours, Earle Ovington, Monoplane 13. PS—some gusty up here. Field below looks fine." When he was done writing, Ovington flew over the judges' stand and dropped his note to Mr. Woodruff.

This airmail delivery was repeated along the same route for another week while the fair went on. On September 26, Postmaster General Hitchcock himself went up as a passenger/mail carrier in a biplane flown by Captain Paul Beck, a thirty-pound bag of mail on his lap. The bags of mail dropped at Mineola often broke open from the force of the drop, but the letters were safely retrieved. From Mineola, the airmail went to Brooklyn for routing to its destination in the usual way. Fifty thousand pieces of mail were carried on planes along that first airmail route during its test period from September 23 to October 1, but only precious few of them still exist today. In 2018, an envelope carried on the first airmail flight sold for $600 at auction.

Postmaster Hitchcock was so encouraged by these first airmail flights that he set up several others around the country. By the end of 1911, airmail flights had taken place in about twenty locations, and Hitchcock requested his department be given $50,000 by the government for further experiments with airmail. From its humble beginnings on the Hempstead Plains, airmail soon became the common, efficient, globe-spanning service that we take for granted today.

The American Aeroplane Supply House in Hempstead manufactured replicas of Bleriot-type monoplanes. On June 30, 1911, Willie Haupt made a twelve-minute flight at an altitude of five hundred feet at the Mineola Aviation Field in one of their machines. The image here dates to 1912 and shows one of their Bleriot-type planes at Garden City.

By 1912, there was a second licensed female pilot in the United States, Mathilde Moisant, sister of the school's founder. Its flying lesson methodology was unique. The school owned several Moisant monoplanes; these were planes that were built in their factory in Manhattan. One of the planes had an engine that was not powerful enough to lift off the ground. This first plane was used for students in a phase called "grass cutting," as the plane just speeds along the runway and the student learns how to control it. Another plane had a slightly better engine that allowed it to hop a few feet off the ground at a time. A third type of plane could make flight not for long and not at a high speed. The fourth and final phase of flight training took place in a standard Moisant monoplane. The instructor never rode with his students; he coached from the ground. The price for a course of instruction was $750 and guaranteed to teach a student until they learned to fly, even if it took six months. For comparison, a brand-new Ford Model T cost $690 in 1912.

By July 1912, there were thirty-five hangars at the Hempstead Plains airfield, with twenty-seven of them rented by several different aviators or flight schools and eight vacant hangars waiting for occupants. Hangars 1 through 5 were concrete; numbers 1 through 3 were occupied by the Moisant School. The Moisant-built field was now the center of Long Island aviation; by the summer of 1912, the Nassau Boulevard Aerodrome and the original Curtiss Mineola field had both been abandoned.

At one point, the Moisant School offered a free Moisant monoplane (without motor) to the student who "makes the best record for least breakage, quickness in learning and general aptitude for flying" by May 15, 1913. In 1914, Moisant military monoplanes were sold to the Mexican government, and the Moisant School trained a dozen Mexican army officers in flying. In April 1914, an aviator named Charles Niles took one of these Mexican-bound planes for a test run from the Hempstead Plains field and rose to an altitude of eleven thousand feet, far surpassing the eight thousand required in the test.

For all its successes, mentions of the Moisant School on the Hempstead Plains cease after 1914, and a 1915 article refers to it as "the old Moisant school," as in "no longer in existence." The outbreak of World War I in Europe led the school's French flight instructors to return to Europe to participate in the war effort. Though the aviation field was still in use by others, it would soon transition to a government training field. In July 1916, the Signal U.S. Army Corps founded the Signal Corps Aviation Station at the Hempstead Plains Airfield to train pilots in the National Guard. Among those training there was Quentin Roosevelt, son of the former president. Once the United States entered World War I in 1917, the Hempstead Plains field centered on training pilots and other airplane crew members for the war effort. The field, also known as the Mineola Aviation Field, was renamed after Second Lieutenant L.W. Hazelhurst, who died in an aircraft accident in 1912. The field was renamed again as Roosevelt Field in honor of Quentin Roosevelt after his death in France in July 1918.

Once the war ended, Roosevelt Field transitioned back to a civilian airfield and the site of Lindbergh's eventual flight. But the amazing Long Island aviation pioneers of 1909–13 had paved the future's way with their brave, record-breaking feats. Their contributions are celebrated today in the Cradle of Aviation Museum in Garden City, but any traces of their existence are long vanished from the sites from whence they once flew their record-breaking missions.

Chapter 12

LOST COUNTRY LIFE PRESS

There are plenty of major companies headquartered on Long Island these days, but back in the early twentieth century when one of the largest and best-known publishers made a sudden move out of New York City, it was unheard of. Doubleday & McClure (soon after Doubleday, Page & Company) was founded in New York City in 1897, and within a year, the company was famous due to its publication of Rudyard Kipling's bestselling book *The Day's Work*.

Because of their success, Doubleday's existing building on 16th Street in Manhattan (built in 1905) was in just a few years already inadequate for their operations; they had a separate stock room on 25th Street, and their books were printed at different locations in the city. The company tried to figure out what to do and decided the most efficient solution would be to have a single large building in which all their operations could be consolidated. According to a little book that Doubleday published in 1913 about their operation, "We needed at least 150,000 square feet of floor space: this meant a building on a plot say one hundred feet square, fifteen stories high, with cellars and subcellars, and much of the space taken up by elevators and service rooms."

But where could they accomplish this? Rents and taxes in New York City made that seem like an unlikely answer. One of the magazines the company published at the time was called *Country Life*, in which they printed articles about the benefits of living in the country. An article about their move explained:

For eight out of ten years of our existence, we have been advocating country life in season and out of season, and now we propose to accept our own advice....After a good deal of investigation, covering all the pros and cons, we have decided that the tendency must be away from the crowded city for making these things which do not, for some good reason, have to be made in the city itself.

The article continued: "By moving to the country we hope to get the best possible working conditions in the way of light and air and pleasant surroundings. But, of course, we have no intention of founding a colony. Our employees decide for themselves where they can conveniently and comfortably live."

In March 1910, Doubleday bought forty acres of land at $600 per acre, a crescent-shaped plot along Franklin Avenue in Garden City, that was a half mile long and five hundred feet deep at its widest and was located adjacent to existing railroad tracks on the Hempstead Branch of the Long Island Rail Road. The newly built Penn Station in Manhattan along with the newly opened railroad tunnel under the East River allowed for quick transportation

The original Doubleday building (1910) still stands on Franklin Avenue.

from Manhattan to Garden City, so they saw it as an ideal location for their operations. They really felt Garden City was "the country" (though Garden City was a well-established village, the building was located just south of the downtown), and so they decided their new printing operation would be called the Country Life Press.

Frank Doubleday hired an architect and had hundreds of plan sheets drawn up for the construction of their new headquarters building and elaborately landscaped grounds. The company was determined to move into the new building in the fall of 1910, so to meet that fast-track schedule, construction had to be done quickly. Supplies were ordered, including millions of bricks and many tons of cement and steel. The steel arrived just four days after being ordered, all the way from Pittsburgh. Railroad spur tracks leading from the newly electrified Hempstead railroad line to their building were laid in a couple of days. There were hundreds of men working on the site at the peak of activity.

The building itself was begun on June 1, 1910, following a slight delay, and at that time it seemed impossible that all could be ready for a move in time for the November issues of Doubleday magazines to be printed in Garden City. Former president Theodore Roosevelt laid the cornerstone for the Doubleday headquarters on August 19, 1910 (as it was a steel frame building, brick work did not begin for a couple of months), and offered some words of encouragement and support for the move from the city:

> *I feel that it is so important more and more to spread the city work out into the country regions. I feel that everything that tends to spread the population as it becomes congested in the great cities, everything that gives more chance for fresh air to the men, the women, and above all, to the children, counts for just so much more in the development of our civic life.*

According to the 1913 Doubleday history book:

> *A large quantity of supplies had to be contracted for, steel, cement, some millions of bricks, and all at break-neck speed, as we had decided that we should move in the Fall of 1910. Many tales could be told of rushed work; steel from Pittsburg being actually delivered on the ground four days after the order was given; cement by the car-load, and trains of brick hurrying along; sand and gravel dug by the thousand yards from a pit on our own land, our own railroad track laid in a couple of days and several hundred men beginning to work all at once.*

Yet somehow, work progressed quickly enough so that the printing machinery could begin being moved to the new site on September 15. On October 1, 1910, the office staff moved to Garden City, though work on the building was still finishing up.

The printing and binding plant, stock rooms and paper storage were all located on one floor. Paper was transferred directly from railroad cars into the building for ease in the printing process. Finished books were transferred to the freight cars from the other end of that floor. When begun, the capacity was fifteen thousand magazines and five thousand books a day, but it soon increased to fifteen to thirty thousand magazines and ten to twelve thousand books daily.

There were tennis courts, a baseball diamond, lawn bowling, a garage, and a restaurant. There was even a grocery store that sold food items including vegetables raised in the Doubleday gardens on site. There was also a 30-by-70-foot, 6-foot-deep Italian pool that was inspired by a pool at a villa near Rome. It was lined by 20- to 35-foot-tall cedar trees brought from various places on Long Island. The 200-by-125-foot court flower garden was designed so that it was continuously in bloom with different seasonal flowers for eight months of the year, from daffodils in April to chrysanthemums in November. It was also laid out such that many of the corporate offices looked out onto it. There was a collection of three hundred varieties of rock and alpine plants, an evergreen garden (150 varieties; many of them were assembled by Hicks Nurseries, see chapter 7), a peony garden, a rose garden, and an iris garden. Two miles of walkways wound through the various gardens. One of the other features of the garden was an intricately designed sundial that celebrated the first century of book printing (1455–1555).

The four-hundred-foot-long building's interior was laid out such that no working spot was more than forty feet from a window. The building used 250 miles of piping and 200 miles of electric wire and 1.5 miles of curtain fabric for the windows. It even had its own post office within the building. There was also a "hospital" for those who fell ill or were injured while at work. Thousands of gallons of water per hour were pumped from wells on the property for use in the building and for the pool and fountains and gardens.

In 1911, Doubleday had the LIRR build a special train station just for its use—Country Life Press, which was just steps away from the rear entrance of the headquarters building, including a brick station house.

An official "housewarming" party for the newly relocated company was held on May 17, 1911. Five hundred guests were invited to the event,

The Long Island Rail Road's Country Life Press station, built for Doubleday in 1911, is still in use today as a passenger stop along the Hempstead line.

brought there by a special train from Penn Station. All departments were open for viewing to the guests, and a tea was served in the gardens outside.

By 1913, the operation had grown from what had been four hundred people in New York City to almost one thousand in Garden City. The company attributed that growth to the favorable conditions in the country versus the city. According to their 1913 book:

> *In New York the clerk and operator must usually travel on an average of two hours a day in the subway or trains in crowded cars between home and work. Men and women get to their tasks tired and return home exhausted at night. In the country, when the home is near-by, they increase their living day (counting the journey as wasted) perhaps 20 percent, and working conditions and comforts at probably 20 percent more.*

The company had a fleet of trucks that could carry a total of eighteen thousand pounds a day.

A 1915 newspaper article detailed some of the process and statistics behind the making of a book at Country Life Press. There were 300,000 copies of a novel by Francis Perry Elliott printed in July and August 1915. The book required 5,563 reams of paper and two or three railcar loads of glue, ink, cloth, and twine to print and bind the books. It took fourteen presses six weeks to print the copies of the book and twelve freight railcars to ship the books to five thousand bookstores around the country. In those days, company founder Frank Doubleday would often wander into the printing press area to watch the books get printed. In November 1915, the company set a new record, binding and delivering 16,000 books in a single day. By this time, they could print 15,000 to 20,000 copies of magazines a day.

Several times a week, parents brought excited children to Doubleday to catch a glimpse of John Martin, the editor of a very popular children's magazine of the time called *John Martin's Book*. In 1916, Doubleday hosted about three hundred editors who were in New York for the National Editorial Association meeting. The company ran a special three-reel film for the visitors, showing the entire process of how books were made, from the delivery of the manuscript to the delivery of finished books to stores.

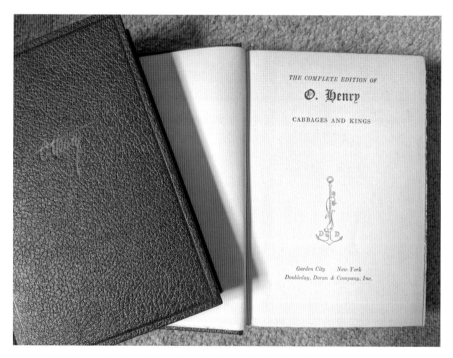

A pair of O. Henry books published by Doubleday in Garden City during the early twentieth century. O. Henry and Rudyard Kipling were two of the big names that made Doubleday famous early on.

During World War I, Country Life Press station was a great help to the thousands of soldiers or their visitors heading to or from Camp Mills (see chapter 14); it was the nearest train station to the camp, which was located just east of the spot.

By 1919, the Country Life Press printing capacity was up to fifty thousand magazines per day and twenty thousand hardcover books a day. Things were going very well for them by this point; they had five hundred books in print, and some were doing exceptionally well. For example, they had sold two million copies of Rudyard Kipling's books and over four million of O. Henry's books.

In 1938, the Country Life Press separated from Doubleday and became an independent printing firm, though still doing Doubleday's printing as well. The extensive gardens were reduced by the need to expand the operations and build more parking spaces. By 1945, the press was capable of printing 115,000 books per day, but by 1958, Doubleday's printing efforts had relocated elsewhere and the plant was converted to office space. In 1980, Doubleday bought the New York Mets baseball team; Nelson Doubleday Jr. (grandson of Frank Doubleday) sold his stake in the Mets in 2002. The old Doubleday headquarters building was sold in 1987, and the company relocated to Indiana. In 2008, Doubleday merged with Knopf Publishing Group to become Knopf Doubleday Publishing Group. That same year, the old headquarters building (today known as 501 Franklin Avenue) sold for $43 million.

The Doubleday building still stands, as an office building, but its interior was gutted and remodeled in 1996 and its exterior modernized (though the beautifully designed entrance and stained-glass windows just above are still intact). To its south, a condominium building was constructed. Many old (but not original) trees and some fine landscaping still grace the property, but not to the lavish extent of its heyday in the 1910s. Scattered picnic tables and benches are reminiscent of the kinds of amenities that were available to the Doubleday employees of long ago. The sundial is gone too; it was removed in 1956 and relocated to Berryville, Virginia. The Country Life Press station is still in operation, but as of 2022, the 1911 station house was considered structurally unsound, closed off and slated for demolition.

Just some of the thousands of books that Doubleday published from Garden City over the course of its seventy-six years there include: *The Gift of the Magi* by O. Henry (1911), *The Art Work of Louis C. Tiffany* (1914), *The Years Between* by Rudyard Kipling (1919), *The Complete Works of Joseph Conrad* in twenty-six volumes (1926), *Of Human Bondage* by W. Somerset Maugham

(1936), *Rebecca* by Daphne Du Maurier (1938) and *The Martian Chronicles* by Ray Bradbury (1950). Many thousands of copies of these well-designed and crafted books still exist in libraries, used bookshops, and home bookshelves across America. They serve as reminders themselves of the glory of the lost Country Life Press.

Chapter 13
LOST EASTERN COASTAL DEFENSE

Forts have been an important component of New York's military defense system since the early days of the colonies. In both peacetime and wartime, the building of ramparts at strategic locations was a critical step in protecting our population from enemy attack by land or water. As soon as New Amsterdam was founded at the southern tip of Manhattan Island in the early seventeenth century, a fort was built by the Dutch settlers to protect its citizens from attack by the English.

Many more New York forts were built in the years after that, especially during the Revolutionary War and the War of 1812 eras and then again during the Civil War, this time to protect not from a foreign enemy but to guard against attack by Confederate ships. If there was a lull over the few decades that followed the Civil War, it was shattered by the Spanish-American War, which brought the defense of our vital interests against possible attack by the Spanish navy to the forefront of military strategists.

Nowhere was this more evident than on Long Island, where several coastal defense forts were established on the little islands to the east of Montauk and Orient Point at the end of the nineteenth and beginning of the twentieth centuries. The hope was that by establishing this perimeter of several points of defense, even if the enemy got past one island, they would still have the guns of another to contend with. If nothing else, ships trying to pass through this island defense system would be slowed down, thus allowing more time for preparations farther west and north. The entrance to the Long Island Sound was a critical (and previously vulnerable) location because it allowed access to coastal Connecticut towns such as New Haven and Bridgeport, as well as all of Long Island and ultimately the big prize of New York City.

The eastern Long Island coastal defense forts that were built, all within a few years of each other, were:

Fort Terry: Located on Plum Island, the 840-acre Fort Terry was built in 1897 and named after Major General Alfred Terry, a Civil War commander. It occupied the whole island except for a 3-acre plot reserved for the lighthouse. *Army and Navy Life* magazine called Fort Terry "one of the most home-like posts" thanks to the Fort Terry Pastime Association, which arranged for shows to keep the soldiers entertained; there were also baseball games at the fort. In the summer of 1916, a month-long training camp was held for boys ages fifteen to eighteen. The cost was fifty dollars including board, ammunition, uniform, and shoes. The government provided tents, blankets, cots, pillows, and weapons. The instructors were army officers. The camp was a success, as 1,200 boys showed up, coming from twenty-four states to participate. Within five months after the camp ended, the Military Training Camps Association had received more than twenty-three thousand applications for the next camp to be held. After World War II, Fort Terry was inactivated. In 1952, the Army Chemical Corps took over the facilities, and in 1954, it went to the Department of Agriculture and served as an Animal Disease Laboratory. In 2013, the government announced plans to sell Plum Island, but in 2020, Congress voted against that idea, opting to conserve the island and protect it from development.

Fort Michie: This fort was located on and comprised the entirety of Great Gull Island, a tiny seventeen-acre island (though not as small as its neighbor Little Gull Island) a couple of miles east-northeast of Plum Island. Both Gull islands had been deeded to the government in 1803 for lighthouse purposes. Camp Michie was an artillery station constructed between 1897 and 1900. It was named after Lieutenant Dennis Michie, who was a fallen hero at San Juan, Cuba, during the Spanish-American War in 1898. Fort Michie was a small complex. As of December 1899, there were thirty-three men stationed there. In 1904, the surgeon stationed at Fort Michie described the medical facilities there: "The hospital at Fort Michie is a temporary wooden structure lined with paper. It has no chimneys, no flues (except for kitchen), no sinks, lavatories, or baths. It is about 4 feet above ground, and this allows free access of the freezing cold of the winter months. It is situated on the most exposed point of Great Gull Island." He requested the construction of a modern brick hospital with a capacity of eight, at an estimated cost of $20,000.

Each island fort had several batteries of guns located at different points to offer protection in different directions. Fort Michie had these batteries, for example: Battery Palmer: two twelve-inch breechloading rifles (1900–48); Battery North: two ten-inch breechloading rifles (1900–17) and one sixteen-inch gun (1923–48); Battery Benjamin: two six-inch guns (1908–48); Battery Maitland with two six-inch guns (1908–48); Battery Pasco with two three-inch rapid firing guns that were operational (1908–48); and Battery 912 with two ninety-millimeter Anti-Motor Torpedo Boat guns (1943–48).

FORT H.G. WRIGHT: Fishers Island was first recognized as an important defensive location as early as 1704, when a signal beacon was erected on Prospect Hill to warn of an approaching enemy. The 306-acre fort was named after Brigadier General Horatio G. Wright, a Civil War veteran. The U.S. government bought 261 acres at the western end of the island in 1898 and immediately built gun emplacements. Fort Wright was the headquarters of the Long Island Coastal Defense System. As of 1924, it served as the coast and heavy artillery training center for the First Corps Area, the New York National Guard, and the West Point Cadets. By the 1920s, the civilian side of Fishers Island had developed into a summer paradise, and the *U.S. Army Recruiting News* said, "It is doubtful if any post in the army can offer as splendid opportunities and advantages as are available to the 'regular' at Fort H.G. Wright, N.Y." Fort Wright was deemed inactive in 1949.

FORT TYLER: Located on the three-acre Gardiner's Island, the fort was established on land given to the U.S. government by the island's owner, John Gardiner, in 1851 for the building of a lighthouse. The fort was built in 1898 and named after Brigadier General Daniel Tyler, a Civil War veteran and the grandfather of Edith Carow, Theodore Roosevelt's second wife. The fort was abandoned in 1924 and purchased by New York State for fifty dollars. It was known as Gardiners Point Park until 1938, when President Franklin Roosevelt established the Fort Tyler Migratory Bird Refuge on the site.

In addition to regularly scheduled training exercises and target practice that was held at these forts, coastal defense exercises on the eastern end of Long Island were held several times during the early twentieth century. These maneuvers were designed to put both "sides" to the test in trying to outsmart and defeat each other with the goal of improving the fort's defenses

Admiral Asa Walker and his staff at Fort Wright on Fishers Island, circa 1899–1900.

Approximately 1,200 uniformed high school age boys heading to Fort Terry on the SS *Montauk* for military training during World War I.

A twelve-inch gun at Fort Wright on Fishers Island.

A gun firing during a West Point field trip to Fort Wright on Fishers Island in 1925.

and the soldiers' capabilities. The objective of the naval fleet was to find ways to get past the island defenses, and the objective of the troops stationed at the island forts was to stop the fleet from advancing. No one was harmed during these exercises, but points were awarded to each side based on their moves and countermoves and "hits" by the artillery and by unarmed mines. For example, a battleship might be given a life of one thousand points, which was subtracted from with every "hit." If a ship lost all its points, it was out of the exercise.

Maneuvers in 1902 involved a naval fleet operating from a base on Block Island and trying to get through the coastal defense system. That exercise featured an early use of searchlights, which were deemed to be somewhat overrated based on the experiences of both sides. Lessons learned included that the lights must be swept low to the water when used and their beams should not cross to avoid creating a dark and invisible area between the beams; the projectors should be hooded on the shore side; and the observers should be at a distance from the lights to prevent them from being blinded by the intense glare. In this 1902 exercise, two ships managed to get through and position themselves in a "dead angle" that was unreachable by the guns of the various forts. The ships had to contend with two types of mines: contact mines that "exploded" on being hit by the vessel and observation mines that were remotely triggered by a soldier observing the ship's position from the fort.

These war games were good preparedness exercises, but they did sometimes subject the Long Island eastern coastal defense to criticism. Major H.A. Reed of the Artillery Corps said this in 1903:

> *It would be difficult to exaggerate in describing the present ineffectiveness of Fort Michie in preventing a "run by" of an enemy's fleet, especially with weather or darkness favoring the attempt, as well as its exposure to enfilade and reverse fire from any point W. of a N. and S. line. With its most important location and a naturally fine site for a powerful armament to resist attempts of this kind, its present condition is a most apt illustration of the tendency of our self-satisfied nation not to prepare for war in time of peace.*

During the Fortification Appropriation Bill hearings in Congress in 1908, Colonel Frederic Abbot of the U.S. Army Corps of Engineers testified about the defense of the Long Island Sound:

> *As the cities on the shores of Long Island Sound became more and more important with the lapse of time, the Board of Engineers decided that*

A 2011 aerial view of Plum Island, former site of Fort Terry. Beyond it lies Orient Point on the North Fork.

it was advisable to throw out an outer line of defenses near the eastern entrance of Long Island Sound, not with the idea of entirely excluding a fleet, but with the idea of making its passage risky so that these smaller cities would not be liable to a naval raid....We must absolutely defend the whole of Long Island Sound because the territory has become so much more valuable than it was twenty years ago. That eastern end is the place that now must be held, formerly it was not considered necessary. The increasing value of the cities upon the Sound have made it a necessity to convert what was formerly a moderate barrier into an absolute stoppage.

In 1913, maneuvers by Admiral Charles Badger's fleet showed some ingenuity. The admiral had a two-step plan to get past the Fishers Island and Great Gull Island defenses. He waited for a night when there was a wind blowing and sent forth his destroyers with their furnaces burning oil that sent a thick cloud of smoke drifting near the Fishers Island forts. The clouds of smoke melded together to form a wall of black smoke such that the island defenses could not see through it, rendering their equipment temporarily useless. The admiral then sent his thirteen battleships forth

Roseate terns in flight at Great Gull Island, former site of Fort Michie. In the distance is Little Gull Island with its lighthouse.

with their searchlights aimed at the guns and range-finding stations at Fort Michie, blinding them and rendering them incapable. Both defenses were thus incapacitated, and the admiral's fleet could pass through unscathed.

As World War I began, the importance of a coastal defense was once again at the forefront of military strategy. The May–June 1917 edition of the *Journal of the United States Artillery* featured an essay by Captain Howard Landers of the U.S. Army (which had won second prize in a competition) of the potential for an enemy invasion and how their goal would be to "reduce the defenses of Long Island Sound as soon as possible, and then concentrate three divisions at New London, two divisions on Long Island, and march on New York City." It is frightening to read such things today, but this was in the minds of the military leaders of the time as a very real possibility. The captain's recommendation to counter such an enemy plan was for a regiment of infantry, two batteries of field artillery, and two platoons of cavalry on Fishers Island; a regiment of cavalry, two batteries of field artillery, and one platoon of cavalry on Plum Island; and a regiment of infantry and a platoon of cavalry in the area of Orient Point.

With the development of increasingly advanced naval warfare capabilities, the advent of military aviation and a declined likelihood of an attack on Long Island, these bases were no longer needed and were closed. Though these forts became obsolete, lost after only a few decades, in their time they served an important role in the coastal defense of the Long Island Sound during a span of years when there was a very real threat of naval invasion.

Chapter 14

LOST CAMP MILLS

By the early twentieth century, Americans were tired of war. In the previous forty years, the country had gone through a deadly Civil War and then the Spanish-American War and the Philippine-American War. The United States was veering toward a more isolationist view on participation in world affairs. By the time the Great War (later known as World War I) broke out in Europe during the summer of 1914, there was no appetite for American entry into the mess, which was looking to be a bigger and more deadly war than ever. Military technology had advanced, and the fighting was certain to impose massive casualties on any country that joined.

Yet in April 1917, the United States declared war on Germany after continued German submarine attacks on American ships. A massive undertaking would be required to train and mobilize hundreds of thousands of drafted and enlisted troops and get them battle-ready. Long Island was an ideal location for an army camp, as it was close to the port of New York, and the Hempstead Plains was perfect, as there was plenty of available flat and wide-open space. The Plains had already been used for military camps twice before, during the Civil War when Camp Winfield Scott was created in 1861 in what would become Garden City; and during the Spanish-American War, when Camp Black was built and named after New York governor Frank Black.

By 1917, the Hempstead Plains was already host to a civilian flying field near the intersection of Clinton and Old Country Roads; this would later become Roosevelt Field (after Theodore Roosevelt's son Kermit, who died during the war), but during World War I, it was converted to military use and was known as Aviation Field or Hazelhurst 1. To its southeast was Aviation Field 2 or Hazelhurst 2 (later Mitchel Field); it was created during the war and remained a military field after the war ended. For the new training camp, the government selected a four-hundred-acre piece of land just to the south and southwest of Hazelhurst 1. The camp was to be called Camp Mills, after a former superintendent of the United States Military Academy at West Point, Major General Albert L. Mills, who died in 1916.

Camp Mills was selected as the site for the mobilization of the Forty-Second or Rainbow Division, the first large military unit to go overseas. The Rainbow Division was composed of members of the National Guard from around the country who had been mobilized by President Woodrow Wilson. The division consisted of soldiers from twenty-six states, a group of men stretching across the country "like a rainbow," according to Major Douglas MacArthur.

Work on the camp began in earnest on August 12, 1917. Construction was done at lightning speed. The camp's infrastructure was built at an amazing pace. For example, on Tuesday, August 16, work was begun on installing a mile of telephone pole line through the center of the camp, a new central office building, and a new switchboard. By Thursday evening, August 18, work was done and phone service was running through the camp. The first troops arrived a few days later, and by then, water pipes and roads had also been laid.

A visitor to the camp reported in August 1917:

> *Camp Mills, when we arrived, looked like a Western mining camp during a gold rush. Thousands of carpenters, thousands of laborers, hurrying about their Jobs; thousands of hammers pounding away at the framework of many new buildings; thousands of feet of lumber piled high awaiting the honor of helping to house some of Uncle Sam's troops.*

Despite that report, the Camp Mills of 1917 was largely a vast city of tents, though there were some wooden buildings as well, mainly used as kitchens and mess halls for the men. By the end of August 1917, thousands of soldiers from Camp Mills were frequent visitors to Hempstead Village, where "merchants are reaping an added income as the men are purchasing and buying things continually," according to an article in the *Hempstead Sentinel*. Reading rooms were established in a couple of the local churches so

On August 16, 1917, 1,500 workers rush to build Camp Mills in time for the arrival of the Rainbow Division, which included the 69th of the New York National Guard, later known as the 165th Infantry.

the men had a place to seek quiet refuge to read books or write letters. Said one of the men, "It is a fine thing to come here and feel our feet resting on a wooden floor, to know that we have a roof over our heads and to enjoy these facilities. The people of Hempstead have treated us better than, in any town we have been in and we feel at a loss as to how best to express our appreciation of the kindness that is shown us here."

A general schedule followed by the arriving soldiers was as follows:

5:10 a.m. First call for reveille
5:20 a.m. Reveille
6:00 a.m. Mess
6:45 a.m. Sick call
7:00 a.m. Drill
10:00 a.m. Recall from drill
11:30 a.m. Non-commissioned officers school
12 noon Mess
1:45 p.m. First call for drill
2:00 p.m. Drill

4:00 p.m. Recall from drill
4:45 p.m. First call for retreat
5:00 p.m. Retreat
6:00 p.m. Mess
9:00 p.m. Tattoo (a military drum performance)
9:45 p.m. Call to quarters
10:00 p.m. Taps (bedtime)

In October 1917, there was a parade at the camp of the 27,000 Rainbow Division soldiers composed of twenty-seven regiments from twenty-seven states. A crowd of 100,000 people was on hand to witness this display of our military prowess before the Rainbow Division men shipped overseas. A typical journey for the men who had finished their training at Camp Mills and were ready to ship out was as follows: from Camp Mills, they got on a train to Long Island City and from there a ferry to Hoboken, New Jersey, from whence they embarked on a ship bound for France.

A November 1917 newspaper article in the *Hempstead Sentinel* proclaimed, "There is still a demand for rooms from out-town people wishing to come

The 165th Infantry arriving at the still-under-construction Camp Mills, August 1917.

to Hempstead during the stay of the soldiers at Camp Mills. People of the village having spare rooms communicate with the Sentinel office and the office will direct inquiries to them."

Several other small items in that same edition of the newspaper give insight into just how much a part of the local Hempstead community the soldiers were and vice versa:

Last Friday night Miss DeBeau of Jackson Street, gave some very interesting readings at a concert and dance given at Jamaica, for troops from Camp Mills, Miss DeBeau has been very generous in entertaining the various-troops from the camp. Having recently recited at a large concert given in the Municipal Building for the Iowa boys.

Chaplain Marsden of the Oregon Infantry stationed at Camp Mills was the speaker at the evening service at the Presbyterian Church, Sunday evening. The song service which begins at seven o'clock is gaining in favor and hundreds of soldiers drop in to take part in this service which precedes the regular evening worship. Following the service refreshments were served in the Y.M.C.A. rooms.

350 members of the 161st United States Infantry (formerly the Second Washington), from Camp Mills were the members of the Woman's Relief Corps of Hempstead. A banquet of ample proportions was served to the soldier visitors by the ladies. Dancing followed. A number of the soldiers entertained with songs and music. It was a jolly party and when it broke up, the men all joined in singing, "Good Night Ladies." The soldiers all cordially thanked the ladies of the Corps for their excellent hospitality. The members of the Woman's Relief Corps thank those who contributed to make the affair a success.

The Hempstead post office was overwhelmed by the surge in both incoming and outgoing mail. An estimated 100,000 letters and postcards were sent from that post office every day by the end of 1917, including lots of money from the soldiers' military pay that was being sent back home.

The approaching winter of 1917–18 proved to be messy, with flooding rains and then intense cold and snow, to which tent living was not suited at all. Many of the tents had no fires, blankets were scarce and many men had to sleep on the bare ground. There were numerous deaths from pneumonia that winter. By early 1918, conditions were bad enough that the remaining

15,000 men at the camp at that time had to be transferred to Camp Merritt, New Jersey. Camp Mills was reopened in March 1918 due to an increased need for American troops overseas. This time, more permanent infrastructure was constructed. In April of that year, the 35th National Guard Division, composed of troops from Missouri, Kansas, and Oklahoma, was stationed at Camp Mills. At that time, there were 25,000 men stationed at the camp. By the fall of 1918, 500,000 men had been trained, equipped, and shipped to their port of embarkation from Camp Mills, with a high of 24,000 in a single day! There were 838 buildings in the camp with a capacity of 26,500 men (50,000 if tents were included). The base hospital was located north of the camp itself, between Washington Avenue and Clinton Road north of Osborne Road. Some of the buildings of the adjacent Mineola Fairgrounds were taken over, and the annual agricultural fair had to be canceled in 1918 because of military presence on the site. The American Library Association visited the Camp Mills base hospital to lend books (carted in by wheelbarrow) to soldiers. In the days before radio or television, books were the main source of entertainment for those who were laid up with nothing else to do. Among the most popular books in 1918 was Willa Cather's *My Antonia* and Booth Tarkington's *The Magnificent Ambersons*.

During the fall of 1918, when it became clear that the war would soon be ending and soldiers would be returning home, Camp Mills once again played an important role. On September 13, 1918, orders were received to build permanent wooden barracks for the debarkation. The new barracks at Camp Mills were two-story buildings made from wood, each one accommodating 66 men. They were heated with coal heaters, lighted with electricity and sealed with plaster board on the inside and had plenty of windows for light and fresh air. Both floors were used for sleeping quarters, and each soldier had an iron spring bed with a mattress and plenty of woolen blankets, according to accounts of the time. All the buildings in the camp were painted dark green with a deep yellow trim. They were completed by November 1918 by armies of carpenters; a total of 8,000 men were employed to build them. The debarkation barracks could house 18,000 men. Some troops traveled a great distance on their journey home; the 13th Infantry traveled twelve thousand miles from the Philippines to get to Camp Mills. Many of those who returned from the war were sick or injured or became sick after arrival. There were 4,000 wounded soldiers in the base hospital as of December 26, 1918. In January 1919, the Salvation Army Hotel was opened at the intersection of Clinton Road and Stewart Avenue. It had ninety rooms and could accommodate up to 150 sleeping guests.

In the fall of 1918, the Hempstead Branch of the Long Island Rail Road was double tracked from Floral Park to Hempstead Crossing in order to handle the troop trains. Over three million soldiers were transported to Camp Mills on long trains of Pullman cars. Trolley cars were run out to Camp Mills from the train station for the accommodation of the men.

The Spanish flu epidemic hit Camp Mills hard, as it was bound to do in any place that involves tight quarters and a high population. In the first two weeks of October 1918, at least forty-five men stationed at Camp Mills died. The camp was under quarantine between October 9 and November 13, 1918 (it was lifted to allow for celebration of the Armistice on November 11, 1918). The first troops to come home after World War I arrived in New York City in November 1918 en route to demobilization at Camp Mills.

As soldiers returned from overseas, local newspapers from their towns published stories informing their families that they had arrived and could be visited. A March 9, 1919 story in the *Troy Times* explained that the 105th Infantry, which included many soldiers from the Troy area, had arrived at Camp Mills and had a meal of bologna, sausage, macaroni, bread, and coffee. Relatives could visit them that coming Sunday, March 11, as many had been issued seventy-two-hour leaves for the weekend. The soldiers of the 105th were expected to remain at Camp Mills through March 20 after undergoing a delousing process.

Eventually, the flow of troops from overseas began to slow to a trickle. As of August 9, 1919, Camp Mills was officially closed. An article in the *Hempstead Sentinel* said:

> *That Camp Mills is to be finally closed will be received here in Hempstead by the business interests with general regret. During the past two years the thousands of troops and visitors passing through here have brought a prosperity little dreamed of a few years back. Many new business houses have opened and will now probably close. Store rents that in many instances have been trebled will again become normal.*

The entire base hospital was empty of patients by early September 1919, and the 1919 agricultural fair could be held. The camp was sold to the Buffalo House Wrecking Company in December 1919 for $327,300, at which time the camp was nearly empty (an earlier call for bids had resulted in prices deemed too low, so Camp Mills was put up for bids a second time). The camp was dismantled and demolished in 1920. Nearly brand-new lumber and other building materials from the dormitories, hospital,

Returned soldiers watching a performance at the Liberty Theater at Camp Mills on January 20, 1919. The 1,600-seat theater was built in twenty-six days at a cost of $96,000. There was entertainment every night, ranging from vaudeville performances to motion pictures.

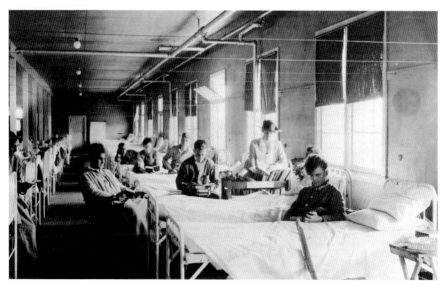

The American Library Association distributed books at Camp Mills for returning soldiers to read. This photograph was taken in the base hospital.

kitchens, and storehouses were used as construction materials for homes being built in Mineola, Hempstead, Baldwin, Freeport, and other nearby communities. As for the Camp Mills site itself, homes were soon built there. The 5,100-square-foot building that was used as a laundry facility for Camp Mills was sold to the Audrey Motors Corporation for use as a manufacturing plant for their touring car called the Audrey – though there are no records of any such car ever having been made. In 1920, the Camp Mills sewer plant became the property of the Village of Garden City. The former Camp Mills neighborhood is now a mix of residential and commercial properties, through which runs Oak Street. The names of the residential streets on which Camp Mills used to sit are pleasant, peaceful names such as Chestnut, Poplar, and Garden Street. The only present-day reminder of the camp's existence is a marker memorializing the Rainbow 269th Division, located on Commercial Avenue and Clinton Road in East Garden City.

Why would there be no trace of this historic site? Why did nobody have the foresight to preserve something as a memento of the war? First, the existing buildings were not suited to the residential purposes that were being considered for the site. Plus, at that time, Americans were quite happy to leave the ugly and deadly war behind. We had defeated the Germans, and that was enough. The war had taken a big toll on the country, and everyone was generally eager to return to civilian life and forget about the last few years of strife. There was no thought to saving anything; demolishing it all suited most people just fine. Just three years after it was built, one of the most important military camps in American history was lost forever.

Chapter 15

LOST WARPLANE FACTORIES

Long Island was not only the cradle of American aviation, but it was also the home of several important military aircraft manufacturers. It started with the Curtiss Aeroplane and Motor Company (founded by pioneer Glenn Curtiss) plant that opened in Garden City during World War I and others in the nearby area and grew from there. With demand for airplanes on the rise after the war, aircraft manufacturers began to open plants on Long Island. With the start of World War II in Europe, the American demand for military planes grew quickly, and Long Island became a hotbed of aircraft production.

In fact, two of the most important World War II aircraft were made in large part on Long Island by the Republic Aviation Corporation in Farmingdale and the Grumman Corporation in Bethpage. The Republic Thunderbolt and the Grumman Hellcat played a large role in the eventual victory of the Allied forces in the war, facing off successfully time and again against Japanese, German, and Italian planes.

Founded in 1931 as the Seversky Aircraft Corporation by a Russian immigrant and World War I pilot named Alexander de Seversky, Republic Aviation was based in East Farmingdale, between Conklin Avenue and the Long Island Rail Road tracks. The Republic P-47 Thunderbolt was first developed during the late 1930s and was officially introduced in May 1941 (just eight months after Republic was given the greenlight to produce them). The army's original order of planes was for fifty-six of these thirteen-thousand-pound aircraft. The plane's production and details were kept secret until just before the first one was ready. It was the first army pursuit airplane to utilize an eighteen-cylinder, two-thousand-horsepower Double Wasp Pratt & Whitney engine that sent it flying at more than 400 miles per hour (and up to 680 miles per hour during a power dive pursuit of an enemy craft). "Designed and produced in record time," read one advertisement, "the 'Thunderbolt' meets every modern requirement in its fire power and protective equipment." It was equipped with eight .50-caliber machine guns (four in each wing).

The manufacture of the Thunderbolt was a complicated process. According to the May 1942 issue of *U.S. Air Services* magazine:

> *Republic uses hydraulic presses to stamp out many of the Thunderbolt's parts. The largest of these presses is a 350-ton Birdsboro, with a 4,500-ton pressure, which women are now manning. Two crews of six keep it in continual service. As soon as the press has shaped a set of pieces, the group that had prepared the set takes it out and immediately starts to put more aluminum in place on the dies. Meanwhile, the group on the other side has just set up another tray of dies, which it now feeds into the press. Each round trip of the press takes only thirty seconds and shapes the parts correct to a thirty-second of an inch.*

The plane and its components underwent rigorous testing. One part of the Republic plant was a three-room "ice box" with twelve-inch-thick walls, in which oils, greases, electric lines, and other plane components were tested at extremely low temperatures to mimic the conditions the plane would face in the stratosphere. Temperatures in the ice box could be lowered to ninety-two degrees below zero, so the researchers had to wear special fishbowl-shaped two-layer Lucite headgear to protect them from the cold. When a Thunderbolt was completed and had been inspected by an army inspector, the plane was ready for action. A pilot would literally get into the finished plane and fly it away into army service.

To prepare for high-altitude flying, the pilots of Republic's P-47 Thunderbolt trained by riding stationary bicycles for half an hour while breathing pure oxygen, right before a flight, to mimic conditions they would face at high altitudes of thirty-five to forty thousand feet and prevent "the bends," the same condition that can affect divers going far below the ocean's surface. The activity removes nitrogen from the bloodstream and thus helps the pilots stay healthy.

A Republic P-47 Thunderbolt flies over Germany in 1945.

Over the course of the war years, more than fifteen thousand Thunderbolts were built, nine thousand of them in Farmingdale. The thirty-five-foot-long plane cost $100,000 to build and took twenty thousand man-hours to make one. They were used on the front lines around the world, including in France, Italy, Germany, India, China, and Japan. According to the January 1943 issue of *Popular Science*, the Thunderbolt's gunpower burst was equal to the impact of a five-ton truck at 60 miles per hour. By the summer of 1944, the newest version of the Thunderbolt had a bubble canopy to offer 360-degree vision, additional horsepower, a top speed of 450 miles per hour, and new propellers to add four hundred feet per minute to the ascent. In the space of thirty days, a single Thunderbolt group was able to cut enemy rail lines in 201 places; destroy six tunnels, ten railroad bridges, and 178 railroad cars; set 226 motor transports afire; blow up seventeen ammunition dumps; set thirty-four buildings and warehouses afire; destroy eleven enemy planes on the ground; sink two barges; destroy a radio station and high-tension tower; eliminate four anti-aircraft posts and three machine gun positions; and damage six landing craft.

Republic continued to produce aircraft after the war ended. As of 1946, the Republic facility in Farmingdale had a total floor area of 1,259,146 square feet. Its main building had 564,000 square feet with clearances of up to 35 feet. The warehouse was 340,000 square feet with clearance of 22 feet. There were twenty-four additional buildings including hangars, office, and administration buildings. There was an airfield adjacent to the facility. The successor to the Thunderbolt was the Thunderjet, which could go six hundred miles per hour. By the 1950s, there was also the F-84F Thunderstreak and the RF-84F Thunderflash. The company was acquired by Fairchild in 1965 and became known as Fairchild Republic. With the waning of the Cold War and a decrease in military airplane orders, however, there were extensive layoffs, and the factory shut down in 1987.

Most of the Fairchild Republic buildings on the ninety-one-acre property were demolished in 1997 to clear space for the massive 3,100–parking space Airport Plaza Shopping Center on the south side of Conklin Avenue and east side of Route 110 in East Farmingdale (home to a Staples, Home Depot, Old Navy, Stew Leonard's and Five Below, among others). As of 2023, there was still a lone Fairchild Republic building on the north side of Conklin Street, abandoned and gutted by fire in 2015. It is the last remains of a once

The last of the old Fairchild Republic buildings stands in ruins on Conklin Avenue in Farmingdale.

formidable industry in Suffolk County. The 40-by-120-foot building, though now a mere skeleton of its former self, is impressive in its size, though it was once part of a much more massive manufacturing complex. Republic Airport, once the aircraft company's own testing field, is adjacent to the former aircraft factory and still operates today.

Grumman Industries (later Grumman Aerospace and now known as Northrup-Grumman) was founded in 1930 by three Long Island men and at first operated out of a garage. When orders started to come in from the U.S. Navy, the company grew, and in 1936, it moved to what was then the semi-rural community of Bethpage, on a plot of land bordering South Oyster Bay Road on the west, from the railroad tracks south to the intersection with Route 107. The Grumman manufacturing complex grew to include several factory buildings, testing facilities, hangars, and runways. Before World War II, Grumman employed 1,500 people; that number went up to 27,000 during the war years.

While the army needed land-based planes like the Republic Thunderbolt, the navy also needed planes that were designed for the war in the Pacific, where the "base" was most likely an aircraft carrier. The Hellcat F6F was an aircraft carrier–based navy plane that was designed based on feedback received in early 1942 from pilots who had flown Grumman's Wildcat airplane against the Japanese during the early days of the war. They wanted a plane with more speed and better ability to climb or "go upstairs faster," as the pilots phrased it; the Wildcat and other army planes had better armor and durability than the Zero but less maneuverability, which could prove to be fatal for the Americans. The thirty-three-foot-long Hellcat, which entered production in May 1942 and first flew in July 1942, was the answer; it was the first plane that was built in response to our experience fighting the dreaded Japanese Mitsubishi Zero airplane. It was the successor to and improvement on the Grumman Wildcat; it was the plane that navy pilots wanted. With a two-thousand-horsepower Pratt and Whitney engine, it could reach speeds of four hundred miles per hour. It had a wingspan of forty-two feet (and its wings could fold, making it easy to store on aircraft carriers when not in use) and retractable landing gear, could reach thirty-five thousand feet in altitude, and was armed with .50-caliber machine guns and six rockets. This aircraft carrier–based navy

Inside the Grumman manufacturing plant in Bethpage, 1940.

A Grumman F6F Hellcat taking off from the deck of the aircraft carrier USS *Bataan* in 1944.

plane saw action for the first time in September 1942 in a raid on Marcus Island. An article in the November 1943 issue of *Popular Science* said the new Hellcat "makes the Wildcat look like a fireside tabby."

The Hellcat was considered the best of the carrier-based fighters. During the first five months of 1944, Hellcats destroyed 767 Japanese planes, 444 in combat and 323 on the ground. The navy kept the orders for the popular plane coming, and a total of 12,275 Hellcats were built by Grumman and delivered to the navy during the war. An article in *Naval Aviation News* proclaimed, "The F6F was a wide-wheeled fighter that Grandmother could fly." In March 1945, Grumman turned out 605 Hellcats in one month, a new world record for output of any airplane from a single plant. The plane was a big success. By war's end, Hellcats had destroyed 5,155 of the 9,249 Japanese aircraft the navy and marines had taken down in combat. The navy's top three aces were all Hellcat pilots.

While the war was still ongoing, Grumman developed two new successor planes, the Bearcat and Tigercat, but the Hellcat remained the dominant force out of the three. Grumman continued to be strong through the Cold War and has played a big role in the space program since 1962, building thirteen lunar modules (one of which is on display at the Cradle of Aviation Museum). The workforce was still twenty-five thousand in 1986, but job cuts left the workforce at just three thousand by 1996, when Grumman announced a huge scale-back and sell-off.

New office buildings, parking lots, grass, and a water tower are now located where the Grumman runway once was. One of the remaining Grumman buildings is now a film studio called Grumman Studios. Opened in 2009, the 460,000-square-foot space was used to shoot films such as *The Amazing Spider-Man 2*, *Annie*, *Marvel Avengers*, *Peter Pan Live*, *The Bourne Legacy*, *Salt*, *Winter's Tale* and *The Sound of Music Live*. An old Grumman radar dome still sits atop the building. Besides the building, one of the most compelling reminders of what once was is a Grumman F-14 Tomcat fighter plane, number 712 out of 712—the last one ever made (it was produced between 1970 and 1992)—which sits near the intersection of Grumman Road West and South Oyster Bay Road, a monument to the glory days of Long Island's military airplane industry.

Chapter 16

LOST WHALING

Today, we don't think twice about flipping on a light switch to turn on a lamp. In the days before electricity, it was not so simple. You could either light a candle or use a lamp that burned some kind of fuel. Back then, whale oil was valuable because it could light lamps in homes and on streets more brightly, reliably, and safely than candles. Because whales are so large, a single whale could provide forty to fifty barrels of whale oil, in addition to whalebone (used to make corsets and carriage whips, among other items), thus making whaling a profitable venture.

In the beginning, the "whaling" that took place on Long Island was done by simply taking advantage of any whales that may have washed ashore. Suffolk County towns recognized the value of the whales and were protective of them. In 1671, the Town of Huntington enacted a law that stated, "It was ordered and agreed with the consent of the whole town, that no foreigner or any person or persons of any other town on this island shall have any liberty to kill whales or any other small fish within the limits of our bounds." In 1687, the whaling stations in the Hamptons produced about 2,250 barrels of whale oil.

By the year 1700, enterprising men were setting out in small boats to search for whales near the southeastern coast of Suffolk County. Their efforts were met with moderate success. In 1726, eleven whales were killed at Southampton. As fewer whales were spotted near the shores, the whaling enterprise shifted to a seagoing one. This included larger ships that were built specifically for whaling and long voyages to the open ocean. Sag Harbor was the island's primary whaling port. By 1807, there were four whaling ships sailing from Sag Harbor, but that number grew quickly; by 1832, there were twenty ships; by 1841, there were forty-four; by 1843, there were fifty-two; and at its peak in 1847, there were sixty-three whaling ships based in Sag Harbor. The thirty-two whaling ships that returned to port that year brought back 3,919 barrels of sperm oil, 63,712 barrels of whale oil, and 605,340 pounds of whalebone.

By the 1830s, whaling had taken hold in several Long Island ports, including Cold Spring Harbor, Peconic, Jamesport, New Suffolk, and Greenport, and it remained an important part of Greenport life through the mid-nineteenth century. As of 1834, there were two whaling ships based out of Greenport; in 1841, there were five whaling ships; and in 1844, there were seven. Whaling was not just done casually by a ragtag group of people; operations were often incorporated for this profitable business. In 1838, the Cold Spring Harbor Whaling Company was formed "for the purpose of engaging in the whale fisheries of the Atlantic and Pacific Oceans and elsewhere, and in the manufacture of oil and spermaceti candles, and in erecting dock accommodations at Cold Spring Harbor."

When ships departed their Long Island ports on a long whaling voyage, it was a big event. Wives and children had to say goodbye to their husbands and fathers, without knowing exactly when (or even if) they would meet again. An article in *The Sailor's Magazine* described an 1844 religious meeting on board a whaling ship that was about to leave (with more spectators on the wharves and other nearby ships) the village of Greenport. Local Presbyterian and Methodist ministers gave sermons along with "Rev. Prof. Carry" from New York City, and there was also singing, reading of Scriptures, and prayers offered for the departing sailors; according to a witness, "the whole scene was, in itself, deeply impressive."

The earlier whaling voyages were in the Atlantic Ocean, but by the early nineteenth century, heavy whale hunting had depleted the Atlantic whale population, and thus the whalers had to go farther afield and for longer journeys. A typical one-year whaling voyage (and most voyages were longer than that) would require the following typical supplies: "60 barrels pork, 60 barrels mess beef, 24 barrels flour, 8,000 pounds bread, 2,500 pounds pilot bread, 400 pounds hams and shoulders, 300 pounds cheese, 700 pounds butter, 7 barrels vinegar, 3 barrels dried apples, 3 bags coffee, 500 gallons molasses, 300 pounds cod fish, and 16 pounds pepper."

Whaling was also a very labor-intensive activity. Besides the crew of between twenty to fifty men, it required numerous support people in the whaling villages and surrounding area to make a voyage happen. Building

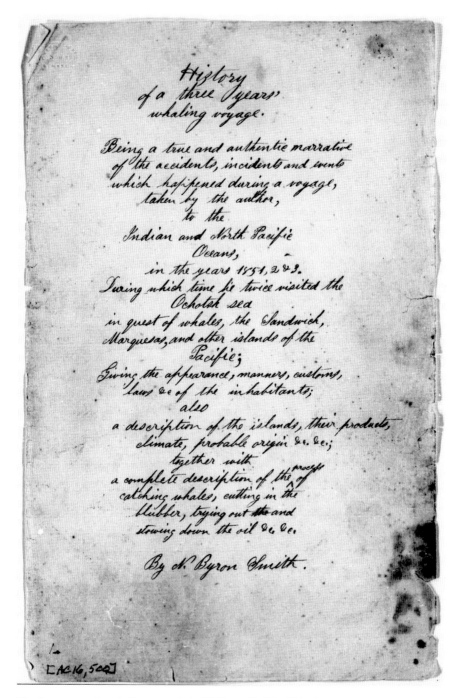

History
of a three years'
whaling voyage.

Being a true and authentic narrative
of the accidents, incidents and events
which happened during a voyage,
taken by the author,
to the
Indian and North Pacific
Oceans,
in the years 1851, 2 & 3.
During which time he twice visited the
Ochotsk sea
in quest of whales, the Sandwich,
Marquesas, and other islands of the
Pacific;
Giving the appearance, manners, customs,
laws &c of the inhabitants;
also
a description of the islands, their products,
climate, probable origin &c. &c.;
together with
a complete description of the process of
catching whales, cutting in the
blubber, trying out the and
stowing down the oil &c. &c.

By N. Byron Smith.

[AC16,500]

The front page of a whaling memoir by N. Byron Smith of his three-year voyage that sailed from Greenport in 1851.

122

a four-hundred- or five-hundred-ton whaling ship itself was a monumental effort, but the work did not end there. Coopers had to make the barrels, and carpenters had to do odd jobs on the ship, as did riggers, caulkers, and blacksmiths. There were sailmakers, whaleboat makers (the smaller wooden craft that were rowed from the ships closer to the whales), dock workers, and clothing makers to make sailors enough clothes to last for one to three years. All told, there were almost seven hundred different kinds of tools, instruments, utensils, and items of clothing and provisions that were taken on a whale ship for a Cape Horn voyage. The total cost of a three-year voyage could run up to an astounding $60,000 for supplies and ship combined. That would be over $2 million in today's currency. Fortunately, with a successful whaling trip, that money would be recouped and then some. Ships did not return after killing one whale; they sought out as many whales as possible to bring home the maximum haul. Success was not always guaranteed; the ship *Splendid*, sailing out of Cold Spring Harbor, was out to sea for more than seven months without getting a single drop of whale oil. In the next two months, however, sailing around the Bering Strait, they brought in two thousand barrels of whale oil.

According to a turn-of-the-twentieth-century book on Long Island:

> The vessels used to set out on their voyages in the Fall and would usually go direct to the port of Honolulu, in the Sandwich Islands. From there they would proceed to the Arctic and remain there during June, July, and August and return to Honolulu again by Sept 1. Then they made a voyage south into the Indian Ocean for sperm whales, which voyage would be called "between seasons" and would last from six weeks to two months. The ships would be absent from Cold Spring Harbor three and sometimes four years. These long absences naturally made the arrival or departure of a ship a most important and stirring event in the little port.

Long Island's whaling villages grew as their whaling ventures expanded. For example, by 1846, there were about one hundred homes and seven hundred residents in Greenport thanks in large part to whaling. The industry continued to grow, and by 1854, there were ten whaling ships based in Greenport. That number went up to eleven in 1856. The whaling ship numbers declined quickly to nine in 1857, seven in 1858, four in 1859, two in 1860, and none in the years after that. Compare this to Sag Harbor, which had twenty whaling ships based there in 1859, a number that declined but was still eight whaling ships by 1866.

A whaleboat on the property of the Whaling Museum in Cold Spring Harbor.

A firsthand account by a whaler who had set off on a voyage from Greenport in the 1850s described what supplies the sailors required:

> *The next day we repaired to the store, where we were furnished with clothing for a voyage of three years; consisting of one straw bed the size of the berths, one quilt and two woolen blankets, which constituted the bedding for each man, then each one was provided a sea chest in which to carry his wardrobe, the principal articles of which were, one coat, one vest, three pairs woolen pants, two pairs duck pants, four over and four under woolen shirts, the same number of drawers, two hickory or cotton shirts, one pair of boots, two pair of shoes, four or five pairs of woolen stockings, two or three hats.*

Long Island whalers sought ways to be more efficient. Thomas W. Roys of Southampton invented several devices during the 1860s, including a shoulder-held harpoon gun in 1861 and an improved rocket harpoon in 1865. In June 1862, he received a patent for his invention titled "Improved Apparatus for the Raising of Dead Whales to the Surface of the Water." This invention featured a ten-foot-long, two-hundred-pound barbed instrument he called a "whale raiser" that was thrust into the whale, which was then raised to the surface.

Whaling was a dangerous venture. The voyages were long and on the open ocean, where disease could strike at any time and without proper medical attention could lead to death. There always lurked the fear of storms that could wreak havoc on a ship, and thrashing whales could overturn or destroy the little whaleboats. Some of the dangers were immortalized in *Moby-Dick*, the fictional account of whaling by Herman Melville, published in 1851 at the peak of American whaling. A Whaler's Monument was erected in 1856 in a Sag Harbor cemetery, featuring a carving of a sperm whale that had struck and wrecked a whaleboat. The boat is upside down with three men hanging on for dear life and holding the dead body of a fourth man. On the monument were carved the names and ages of six shipmasters who died between 1838 and 1846, all under the age of thirty. Written on the monument is the following: "To commemorate that noble enterprise, the Whale Fishery; and a tribute of lasting respect to those bold and enterprising Ship Masters, sons of Southampton, who periled their lives in a daring profession, and perished in actual encounter with the monsters of the deep. Entombed in the ocean, they live in our memory."

James Fenimore Cooper wrote in his novel *Sea Lions*, published in 1849:

> *As a whaling town, Sag Harbour is the third or fourth port in the country, and maintains something like that rank in importance. A whaling haven is nothing without a whaling community. Without the last, it is almost hopeless to look for success. New York can, and has often fitted whalers for sea, having sought officers in the regular whaling ports; but it has been seldom that the enterprises have been rewarded with such returns as to induce a second voyage by the same parties. It is as indispensable that a whaler should possess a certain esprit de corps, as that a regiment, or a ship of war, should be animated by its proper spirit.*

Just a few years after its peak on Long Island, by 1860, whaling began to rapidly decline. According to a 1913 address given in Cold Spring Harbor on the history of whaling there, "Whales were becoming scare and shy; cargoes were to be obtained only by very long and hazardous voyages." Besides this, there were other several factors behind the decline of whaling, including the discovery of petroleum in Pennsylvania in 1859, which served as a more efficient and readily available substitute for whale oil. The start of the four-year-long Civil War in 1861 also put a damper on whaling efforts, between the danger of whaling ships being targeted by Confederate vessels and the general refocusing of priorities to the war effort. In addition, around this time, Norwegians discovered more effective whaling methods that were not cost effective in the United States. Then in 1880, Thomas Edison

The Whaling Museum in Sag Harbor is housed in an 1845 building that was the home of Benjamin Huntting II, wealthy owner of whaling ships.

patented the electric light bulb, which meant no more need for whale oil lamps. Whaling, which continued to a lesser extent elsewhere in the country during the twentieth century (the oil was used in hydraulics and the meat for livestock food), was finally banned by the United States in 1971 as many species of whale were declared endangered.

Though whaling is long gone on Long Island, there are still readily accessible mementoes. Several of the coastal towns on Long Island were largely built on the success of whaling, and many of the nineteenth-century buildings in places like Sag Harbor, Cold Spring Harbor, and Greenport built by whaling captains or merchants who thrived due to whaling still stand today; the villages themselves are vestiges of the island's whaling heritage. While there is no chance of finding items such as whale oil lamps in modern everyday life, these scarce items are preserved in Long Island's two whaling museums: the Cold Spring Harbor Whaling Museum, which opened in 1936 and has a collection of six thousand whaling-related items; and the Sag Harbor Whaling Museum, which opened in 1945 in the mid-nineteenth-century home of a merchant whaler.

Chapter 17

LOST LIFE-SAVING SERVICE

B efore the advent of precision navigational systems, lighthouses were the main defense against shipwrecks, warning captains to steer clear. Lighthouses, though helpful and placed at strategic locations around the island, were not enough to prevent tragedy. Shipwrecks were nevertheless commonplace along the coast of Long Island. All types and sizes of ships sailing to New York from ports around the world fell victim to several culprits ranging from stormy seas to rocks or sandbars, and hundreds of lives were at risk every year. Most shipwrecks did not occur miles away from land and were not due to fire or explosions or any dramatic system failures. Most shipwrecks were due to ships striking rocks, reefs, and sandbars a few hundred feet to a few miles from land and usually in severe weather when the seas were rough, winds were fierce, or fog was thick. Ships would get off course and run aground. The danger lay in trying to get the passengers and crew off the disabled vessel and back to shore, which was often quite nearby. When survivors took matters into their own hands, the results could be deadly because they did not have a true idea of exactly where land was.

Unfortunately for those on wrecked ships, well into the nineteenth century there was still no organized system on Long Island to provide them with assistance, and so many lives were lost. One of the worst nineteenth-century tragedies was the British sloop-of-war *Sylph*, which got lost in the fog and was wrecked off Southampton in 1815, and only 6 of the crew of 133 survived. In November 1836, the *Bristol*, sailing from Liverpool, was grounded during a storm a half mile off Far Rockaway, and giant waves hit and drowned many of the passengers. It was not until the next day that a boat from the shore was able to reach the ship and carry the survivors back to land. Coincidentally, the *Mexico*, another ship leaving from Liverpool just a week after the *Bristol*, was also wrecked off Long Island after a long and harrowing sixty-nine-day voyage across the ocean. Severe weather prevented the ship from approaching land near New Jersey, and it went east and struck a sandbar on January 2, 1837, off the coast of Long Beach ten miles from the wreck of the *Bristol*. The temperature was below zero, and the 16 crew and 112 passengers (Irish immigrants) were freezing after icy water flooded the ship.

On January 3, 1837, a wrecking master (someone who salvages shipwrecks) named Raynor Rock Smith and three of his sons dragged a boat across the frozen bay and then launched the boat into the icy ocean water in an attempt to rescue some of the survivors of the wreck of the *Mexico*, which was visible as it was only about three hundred yards from the shore. They were able to get the captain, 4 passengers and 3 crew members into their boat and safely back to shore, but night was falling, and the cold combined with the tide would make it near impossible to return to the ship. That night, 116 people froze to death in the ice-filled wreck, just a few miles from the port they had been attempting to reach after their long voyage. A couple of months later, Raynor Smith was given a silver tankard by a committee of citizens from New York City in recognition for his lifesaving efforts. He and his crew were also given a $350 reward by the rescued captain. In the speech honoring him, a committee member said:

> *We cannot forget the morning of that eventful day, when the weary* Mexico, *with an insufficient and mutinous crew, doomed to avoidable destruction, poured out her signal gun of distress among the breakers of Long Island; when mothers and sisters and rough sailors stretched imploring hands to the shore and screamed unavailing prayers to Him who rules the storm; when, as if to turn into mockery the attempt to save the predestined ship, violence was given to the winds and fury to the waves, and builded between the vessel and the shore a wall of floating ice, which scarce even hope itself could struggle to surmount.*

In reply, Raynor Smith said, "I thank you, I sincerely thank you for your gift. In return for it I can only say that should a similar wreck, or any other wreck, ever again occur on our shores, I shall endeavor to show that I deserve it."

Though Smith's efforts were valiant and his intentions were good for future lifesaving efforts, it was simply not enough to rely on salvagers or Good Samaritans who happened to be in the area to attempt rescues of shipwrecked passengers and crew. Saving as many lives as possible would require both manpower and the right equipment, and the effort had to be preventive as well as reactive. This was the case all along the coastline, not just on Long Island.

In 1848, Congress passed a bill that provided funds for "surf boats, rockets, carronades, and other necessary apparatus for the better preservation of life and property from shipwreck." The bill originally covered only the New Jersey coastline, but in 1849, Congress appropriated additional funds for the construction of lifesaving stations on Long Island. The first local ones were built that same year at Amagansett, Bellport, Eatons Neck, Fire Island, Southampton, Moriches, Point Lookout, and Quogue. More stations were to follow in the years to come at other locations on the north and south shores, including Blue Point, Georgica, Gilgo, Jones Beach, Kings Point, Napeague, and Shinnecock.

Lifesaving equipment and stations in which to house them were a start, but experienced and official personnel were needed to man the stations and use the equipment, rather than untrained volunteers. As of 1854, station keepers were hired but there were no paid crews to help man the stations. While many lives were saved by volunteers using this equipment, because the government maintained no control over the equipment, it was sometimes subject to misuse. In one case, people were using a lifeboat for mixing mortar. In the winter of 1870–71, several fatal shipwrecks led Congress to appropriate more money and begin a thorough investigation of conditions.

The 1871 investigation of the existing Long Island stations revealed their inadequacy. A report summarizing the findings explained, "Most of the stations were too remote from each other, that the houses were dilapidated, many being so far gone as to be worthless, and the remainder being in need of extensive repairs and enlargement.…The apparatus was rusty for want of care, and some of it ruined by the depredations of vermin and malicious persons." The inspection also found that some station keepers were too old for their duties, some lived too far away from their stations, and only a few were competent at their jobs.

In response to this information, the government established the U.S. Life-Saving Service and provided funds for manning every station with a professional crew. An attorney named Sumner Increase Kimball was placed in charge of the newly established agency and helped it to develop

S.I. Kimball, founder of the Life-Saving Service and general superintendent from 1871 to 1915.

into a respected organization. Standards were established that made for a much more efficient means of saving lives. Each station was manned by a qualified keeper, along with a paid crew of five to assist. As of 1876, the keeper's salary was $200 per year. The Life-Saving Service was broken into geographical districts, and each district had a superintendent who oversaw the operations of all the stations in that district.

The crews of each station patrolled the shore four times a day, two to four miles on either side of their station, to look for ships in danger or needing assistance. In fog, the crews were to patrol the shores all day. The lifesaving stations were stocked with dry clothes, coffee, and food to offer the survivors who were brought back to shore. They had a variety of equipment for rescue operations, medical supplies to offer first aid for minor injuries, and cots to allow survivors to rest before moving on to their destinations. All the equipment, furnishings, and tools within each station were paid for by the government—everything from pillows and blankets to lanterns and ladders.

An 1881 U.S. government book called *Instructions to Mariners in Case of Shipwreck with Information Concerning the Life-Saving Stations Upon the Coasts of the United States* gave some precautionary instructions to captains of ships regarding what to do in case of a wreck and how the Life-Saving Service operates:

> *Each patrolman carries Coston signals. Upon discovering a vessel standing into danger he ignites one of these, which emits a brilliant red flame of about two minutes' duration, to warn her off, or, should the vessel be ashore, to let her crew know that they are discovered and assistance is at hand. If the vessel is not discovered by the patrol immediately after striking, rockets, flare-up lights, or other recognized signals of distress should be used. If the weather be foggy, some recognized sound signal should be made to attract attention, as the patrolman may be some distance away at the other end of his beat.*
>
> *Masters* [ship's captains] *are particularly cautioned, if they should be driven ashore anywhere in the neighborhood of the stations, to remain on board until assistance arrives, and under no circumstances should they*

attempt to land through the surf in their own boats until the last hope of assistance from the shore has vanished. Often when comparatively smooth at sea a dangerous surf is running which is not perceptible four hundred yards off shore, and the surf when viewed from a vessel never appears as dangerous as it is. Many lives have been lost unnecessarily by the crews of stranded vessels being thus deceived and attempting to land in the ship's boats.

Ship's crew were also instructed that it could take several hours from the time they saw a signal from the shore to the time when the rescue vessel arrived because the patrolman would have to return to the station (which might be a few miles away) to get the equipment.

These instructions were issued because they were important to follow; unfortunately, as many of the ships that were wrecked were not American, they likely did not have copies of this manual on board. One of the many shipwrecks that the Life-Saving Service on Long Island assisted with was the Norwegian steamer *Gwent*, which was stranded in March 1901 off Long Beach. The station patrol there sent a surf boat out immediately upon discovering it was stranded. When they arrived in very rough seas, they found one of the ship's boats that had just been launched with four passengers in it. They transferred the passengers to the surf boat and advised the rest of the people to remain on board the ship until morning. Had the ship's boat attempted to make land on its own, it could have easily been carried out to sea.

A lifesaving crew had a few options for rescuing people from a wreck. The first and simplest was launching a lifeboat or surf boat out to the stricken vessel to rescue its crew and passengers. If that type of rescue was not possible, then either a breeches buoy or life car was used. Both devices utilized a rope or cable line that was fired by a special gun and then attached to a stable part of the wrecked ship. The buoy was basically a life preserver with a harness that allowed one person at a time to be pulled back to shore along the cable (same principle as a zip line). The life car was an enclosed metal flotation device that could fit four to six people inside, enclosed with a hatch and thus unaffected by rough seas, also pulled along via the rope back to shore.

The book *Instructions to Mariners* told the ship's crew what to do once the cable line was shot to the wreck:

Make the shot-line fast on deck or to the rigging to prevent its being washed into the sea and possibly fouling the gear. Take particular care that there

A painting by Winslow Homer called *The Life Line* (1884) shows a dramatic sea rescue using a breeches buoy.

are no turns of the whip line round the hawser before making the hawser
fast. Send the women, children, helpless persons, and passengers ashore first.
Make yourself thoroughly familiar with these instructions, and remember
that on your coolness and strict attention to them will greatly depend the
chances of success in bringing you and your people safely to land.

The service was very active because wrecks were commonplace on Long Island. Between 1894 and 1903, 200 vessels were stranded on the Atlantic Ocean coast of Long Island, 114 vessels stranded on the Long Island Sound coast, and 6 more in Gardiner's Bay. The lifesaving station crews did not wait for tragedy to strike; they practiced using the equipment so they were ready for a real wreck. Because wrecks usually happened in bad weather, it was usually not so simple to mount a rescue attempt. In August 1893, the bark *Martha P. Tucker* was wrecked at Long Beach during a hurricane. The vessel was only two hundred yards from the beach, but the lifesaving crew had trouble getting their cart into position. Three women who happened to be at the station helped the crew, and they got the lifesaving equipment in place. A hawser line was successfully shot to the ship, and eleven of the twelve crew members were rescued. The three women later received gold medals for their service from the Maritime Association of the Port of New York.

As of 1901, there were thirty-three lifesaving stations on the coast of Long Island. A 1901 issue of the *Home Magazine of New York* described the lifesaving station at Point Lookout:

> *There are six rooms on the first floor of the government house. In the front and largest room is the lifeboat, mounted on a four-wheeled truck, and in a corner is a life car and the breeches buoy. In a small room adjoining is the Lyle gun, mounted on a two-wheeled carriage, the wreck ordnance and line-throwing appliances, blocks and bushings, signal flags, lanterns, Coston lights, lines, ropes, and cables. To the rear is the large living room, with its cookstove, table and wooden chairs. Here the men cook and eat and lounge and read and smoke. In the wings on either side are the keeper's office, the pantry, and the storeroom, where rubber boots and oil-skin coats and hats hung in a picturesque row upon the wall.*
>
> *There are four watches, or patrols, the first from 4 P.M. to 8 P.M., the second from 8 P.M. to midnight, the third from midnight to 4 A.M., and the fourth and last from 4 A.M. to 8 A.M. The crew take turns on watch, the man who has the first watch also making the fourth patrol. The most arduous and disagreeable watch is that which begins at midnight. As*

A turn-of-the-twentieth-century view of the lifesaving station in Point Lookout.

the clock strikes, two of the guards come from their warm beds up stairs, rubbing their eyes and yawning, moving noiselessly in their stockinged feet. They don their boots, oil-skin coats, and storm hats, and with a Coston light in their hand, sally forth in the night and darkness. Imagine, if you can, the pleasures of this game on a winter's night, with a blizzard raging and the thermometer below zero.

One man goes west along the beach, his eyes always scanning the horizon seaward, looking for a vessel in distress. At the end of his beat he meets another surfman, who comes from the Long Beach station, and they exchange brass checks as an earnest and a proof of their duty done, and then begins the long tramp back to the station.

The Life-Saving Service eventually became outdated. With the advent of motorboats, the means of saving lives changed drastically, and a lot of the old equipment was rendered obsolete. In 1915, the U.S. Revenue Cutter Service was merged with the U.S. Life-Saving Service and renamed the U.S. Coast Guard. In 1939, the U.S. Lighthouse Services was merged with the Coast Guard, further consolidating the ship-saving efforts into one agency. Over the course of its existence across the country, the Life-Saving Service had saved an incredible 186,000 lives due to the efforts of its capable and dedicated crews.

Several of the old Long Island lifesaving stations survive today, but these are later versions, not the original mid-nineteenth-century buildings. Some of them have been relocated and are now in private hands. Others exist where they can be easily seen. A 1934 version of the Point Lookout station house was bought by the Point Lookout Community Church and is part of that structure. An 1872 Babylon lifesaving station is now the Oak Beach Community Center. The Eaton's Neck station is still active, operating out of a 1938 vintage building.

Though the Life-Saving Service is long gone, its spirit lives on in today's Coast Guard, as well as the hundreds of lifeguard stations on Long Island beaches, also dedicated to preserving and rescuing lives when necessary.

Chapter 18

LOST MARINE THEATER

Long Island's Jones Beach State Park has been a beloved local fixture since it first opened in August 1929. The beach was largely the creation of New York's well-known planner Robert Moses, who became president of the Long Island State Parks Commission in 1924. Construction of Jones Beach began in 1926 and was a massive public works undertaking that saw the transformation of an undeveloped and uninhabited barrier island several miles from the mainland into the best-known beach on Long Island. Building it involved filling in of marshes, the use of forty million cubic yards of sand and the planting of dune grass to prevent the sand from blowing away, construction of a lengthy boardwalk, the building of parking lots for tens of thousands of cars and the construction of parkways and bridges to get people from points north to this isolated area.

Besides the miles of oceanfront beaches, among the park's other features are its buildings, including an obelisk-like water tower, two massive Art Deco bathhouses, and other similarly styled buildings. One of its most interesting features was an outdoor theater venue that first opened in 1936. It was literally a marine theater because the stage was an island surrounded by water. The original Jones Beach Stadium was meant as a temporary structure and was of a rather inelegant design, with perpendicular sets of bleacher seating facing the stage in the bay, which was accessible to the performers by a long walkway; from appearances, most seats did not offer an ideal view of the stage at all.

According to an article in the *Sea Cliff News* in June 1936:

> *The Jones Beach Stadium consists of 10,800 seats for spectators, built along the edge of the dock in Zachs Bay, with a stage entirely surrounded by water, which is 136 feet wide and 86 feet deep. Two large pylons 25 feet high and set 100 feet apart on the stage provide a proscenium arch which will frame the scenes depicted in the operas. Four massive pylons at regular intervals will carry the painted scenery, each piece of which is made for triple folding. By rotating the pillars and by unfolding the scenery on the different sides of the pylons, the changes of background are effected. The same principle applies to the bridges and arches which will be used.*

During the mid- and late 1930s, the theater was filled with spectators to see a range of theatrical productions. The early offerings were only for a week or two, so audiences had a range of different options over the course of a single summer. Some of the first shows were operas; *Carmen* by Bizet and *Aida* by Verdi ran on back-to-back nights in June 1936. In August of that year, a show called *My Maryland* (which had run on Broadway for

The Jones Beach Marine Theater in its original configuration, seen here in a 1936 aerial view.

312 performances back in the 1920s) ran, followed by *Countess Maritza*, an operetta by Emmerich Kálmán, a couple of weeks later. One of the offerings in July 1937 was *Frederika*, a new operetta by Franz Lehar. In August 1937, ten thousand people were turned away from a sold-out performance of a show called *Of Thee I Sing*. Tickets in the 1930s were generally available for twenty-five cents, fifty cents, seventy-five cents, and one dollar for the best seats.

In 1937, the Long Island State Parks Commission took a survey of the cars entering the stadium parking field to find out where the viewers were coming from. The results were surprising in how relatively few of the patrons were from Nassau County: Nassau County, 30 percent; Manhattan, 24 percent; Queens, 16 percent; Brooklyn, 12 percent; Suffolk, 10 percent; Bronx, 2 percent; Westchester, 1 percent; other New York counties, 1 percent; states other than New York, 4 percent.

In 1938, one of the most popular musicians of the day, clarinetist, composer, and orchestra leader Benny Goodman, appeared at the Jones Beach Stadium with his swing orchestra and special guests including Lionel Hampton and Harry James.

The shows took full advantage of the marine setting and the lagoon, often using boats and swimmers. In the summer of 1941, for example, the Jones Beach Magic Water Ballet presented an aquatic circus ballet, featuring divers and water clowns. Attractions included the Honey Family, tumbling and acrobatics; Pensy, the horse; the Loyal Stallions, a trained dog act; and an aquaplaning and water-skiing troupe. The marine circus was followed by fireworks.

By 1945, however, the theater was rundown and structurally unsound after being hit by storms over the years. Moses decided to have it razed and build a new one. It was demolished in 1946, but the new and improved marine theater was not completed until 1952. It was built with state funds at a cost of $4.2 million. The stage was still separated from the seats by a lagoon, but it was now expanded and more grandiose, and the seats were arranged in a new semicircular arena-style configuration that allowed for much better views of the stage. One of the first events at the stadium was Olympic trials. Eleven players of the water polo team to represent the United States at the 1952 Summer Olympics were selected at the Jones Beach Stadium during a competition; seven players were picked from the winning team and four from all the other teams.

Aside from an occasional special event, the new theater was primarily used for musical extravaganzas. For many years, Robert Moses had a partnership with Canadian-born bandleader Guy Lombardo, who, along with his band the Royal Canadians, had the role of house musician and also helped to select, develop, and produce the summer's shows. Lombardo was widely known for his New Year's Eve radio and television broadcasts (he was the original Dick Clark/Ryan Seacrest) from 1929 until 1976. He was also well known to Long Islanders during the 1950s and '60s for his East Point House seafood restaurant in Freeport (it burned down in 1970).

Lombardo, often working with his brothers, never disappointed Jones Beach audiences. Pilots were requested to avoid flying over the venue between 8:00 p.m. and 11:00 p.m. so the audience did not miss hearing any of the music or dialogue. The 1954 show was *Arabian Nights*, and it was advertised as "the fabulous spectacle that is breaking all records." The year 1958 saw a musical called *Song of Norway*, based on the life and music of composer Edvard Grieg, which featured one hundred actors, singers, dancers, swimmers, and skaters performing in a reproduction of the village of Bergen, Norway. This was one of the most elaborate sets ever constructed for the venue; one of the set pieces was a sixty-nine-foot Viking ship. Among the other attractions of the show was an ice show performed on an ice rink mounted on a floating iceberg.

In 1961, *Paradise* was debuted, a Hawaiian musical fantasy that included a ninety-foot waterfall, a volcano that erupted, outrigger canoes, a catamaran, and other boats, as well as Hawaiians entertaining the audience with knives and flames and hula hoops.

The year 1963 saw the debut of *Around the World in 80 Days*, based on the popular book by Jules Verne. It featured a lagoon, boats, a train, a balloon, a camel, and an elephant. It cost $1,250,000 to put on the show. It ran 138 performances over two seasons and was seen by about 500,000 people.

For the 1965 season, in a show called *Hit the Deck*, Guy Lombardo and his band made a grand entrance on a sixty-five-foot sailboat. There was also a speedboat race with boats reaching up to seventy miles per hour. According to Lombardo, "The big scenic attraction will be a huge model of a battleship with 32-foot guns that will swing around and face the audience. We resisted the temptation to have them fire for fear of scaring people out of their seats."

In 1966, the theater offered a Mardi Gras–themed show starring Louis Armstrong and his All Stars. The show had also run in 1965 but without Armstrong. The other stars of that show were an eighty-seven-foot pirate ship and a 1,500-pound glittering chandelier. The show did very well with the beloved Armstrong in it, and one Saturday night sold out all 8,200 seats

The reconstructed Jones Beach Marine Theater put on spectacular productions, mostly produced by and featuring popular musician and bandleader Guy Lombardo. This 1954 program is for that summer's production of *Arabian Nights*.

along with an added 226 chairs. A highlight of 1967's revival production of *Arabian Nights* was a ninety-foot-long motor-driven whale.

In 1969 and 1970, the offering was *South Pacific*, and according to its advertisements, it featured "the music we all love...even an honest-to-goodness, full size, actual Navy Landing craft in the Lagoon." Tickets were $3.00, $4.50, and $5.90.

The Marine Theater drew a total crowd of about 375,000 people every summer, except for 1955, when there were five hurricanes in the area and the theater was closed for much of August. Live theater could be an acoustic challenge for the performers. According to a review in the *New York Post* in 1957, "The vastness of the Jones Beach arena can swallow up an actor's performance. There must be an artistry in a performer, a powerful range in a singer's throat, to match the greatness in the area of the theater."

As audience tastes changed (and with Guy Lombardo's passing in 1977), music concerts became more desired than operas and musicals. In 1983, a slate of pop music for Jones Beach included Elvis Costello, Eric Clapton, James Taylor, Chicago, Kool and the Gang, America, Poco, and The Beach

A June 2022 concert at the latest version of the venue, the Northwell Health at Jones Beach Theater.

Boys. The changing use of the theater meant that the water no longer played a starring role; without a need for boats or floating icebergs, there was little purpose for water. People at rock concerts want to get as close as possible to the stage. In fact, one of the problems that happened when popular music concerts began to replace musicals was that people jumped into the water and tried to swim to the stage. Some of the acts appearing in 1991 included Bad Company, Miles Davis, Wynton Marsalis, the Robert Cray Band, Don Henley, Stevie Nicks, Yes, and Jimmy Buffett. In 1992, concert promoter Ron Delsener led major renovations to the theater that filled in the moat and replaced it with seats to create the current iteration, in which the seats go all the way to the stage, eliminating the concept of the stage as an "island." In 1999, a $22 million balcony was added to the theater. Hurricane Sandy damaged the theater, but it reopened in May 2013 after $20 million in renovations.

Attending shows at this venue is still a very "marine" experience given the beautiful water as a backdrop. The theater's name as of 2023 is the Northwell Health at Jones Beach Theater, but it has had several brand-name sponsors over the years, including Tommy Hilfiger and Nikon. The theater currently hosts about twenty-five to thirty concerts per summer. In 2023, it featured twenty-seven concerts including James Taylor, Big Time Rush, Sting, Smashing Pumpkins, and Luke Bryan. While still a maritime experience, it is indeed hard to imagine the most fanciful lost marine version of the venue, with its lavish island stage and front rows composed of water instead of seats.

Chapter 19

LOST PRESIDENTIAL PRESENCE

George Washington

L ong Island has been visited by many presidents over the course of the centuries, but perhaps its most distinguished visitor was none other than the very first leader of the country, George Washington. The first American president set out on a five-day, 160-mile trip across the island in April 1790 (averaging about twelve to fourteen hours of travel per day), just a year after he took office. The tour was especially meaningful in a place that had been occupied by the British for most of the long Revolutionary War, as prior to being elected president, Washington was the general who led the Americans victoriously through the war. It was in a sense a victory lap for the new president.

It was not his first tour of his country as president, nor was it his last; he toured New England in 1789 and the southern states in 1791. But it was certainly his easiest. During the first couple of years of the republic, the federal capital was in New York City, so a visit to Long Island was relatively simple. On April 20, 1790, Washington crossed the East River by boat to Brooklyn (having previously sent across his servants, horses, and carriage) and then made his way to Jamaica, Queens. The places he passed and stopped at in today's Nassau and Suffolk Counties are as follows, with excerpts from his actual diary included in italics:

1) Washington left Jamaica the morning of April 21 and passed through the **Hempstead Plains**.
"The morning being clear & pleasant we left Jamaica about eight o'clock, & pursued the Road to South Hempstead, passing along the South edge of the plain of that name—a

George Washington slept here—he really did, on April 21, 1790. Sagtikos Manor in Bay Shore was home to Judge Isaac Thompson when Washington visited but is now home to the Sagtikos Manor Historical Society, which offers tours of the three-century-old mansion.

plain said to be 14 miles in length by 3 or 4 in breadth without a Tree or a shrub growing on it except fruit trees (which do not thrive well) at the few settlements thereon. The soil of this plain is said to be thin & cold, and of course not productive, even in Grass."

2) In **Hempstead**, he stopped at a tavern that is believed to have been located at the corner of Fulton and Main Streets.

"We baited in South Hempstead, (10 miles from Jamaica) at the House of one Simmonds, formerly a Tavern, now of private entertainment for money."

3) From there, the president's entourage headed south five miles to the Merrick/Freeport area, close to the water, and then east, where he stopped at **Ketchum's in Amityville** to dine.

"We dined at one Ketchum's which had also been a public House, but now a private one—received pay for what it furnished—this House was about 14 miles from South Hempstead & a very neat and decent one."

4) He continued along the road to the **house of Judge Isaac Thompson at Sagtikos Manor**, where he spent the night. The house, built in 1697 and still standing, is today a museum.

"After dinner we proceeded to a Squire Thompson's such a House as the last, that is, one that is not public but will receive pay for every thing it furnishes in the same manner as if it was."

5) and 6) On the morning of April 22, Washington continued east for about eleven miles to the **Greene farmhouse in Sayville**. He continued on to **Hart's Tavern in Brookhaven**, on the north side of the Montauk Highway (Route 80).

"About 8 o'clock we left Mr. Thompson's—halted awhile at one Greens distant 11 miles and dined Harts Tavern in Brookhaven township, five miles farther. To this place we travelled on what is called the South road described yesterday, but the country through which it passed grew more and more sandy and barren as we travelled Eastward."

7) Next, he traveled north to and through Coram on his way to Setauket. Along the way, he crossed through the **Pine Barrens**, with which he was not impressed.

"The first five miles of the Road is too poor to admit Inhabitants or cultivation being a low scrubby Oak, not more than 2 feet high intermixed with small and ill thriven Pines."

8) Passing through Coram, but apparently not stopping, Washington had a couple of observations.

"Within two miles of Koram there are farms, but the land is of an indifferent quality much mixed with sand. Koram contains but few houses—from thence to Setaket the soil improves, especially as you approach the Sound; but it is far from being of the first quality."

9) In Setauket, he stopped at the **inn of Captain Austin Roe** (Main Street and Bayview Avenue; it was demolished in 1936). He passed through the Pine Barrens along the way and described it.

"…to the House of a Capt. Roe, which is tolerably decent with obliging people in it."

10) Now heading west again on his way back to New York City the next morning, April 23, Washington stopped at the **Widow Blydenburgh's in Smithtown** (demolished in 1907).

"About 8 o'clock we left Roe's, and baited the Horses at Smiths Town at a Widow Blidenberg's a decent House 10 miles from Setalkat."

11) He proceeded to the **Widow Platt's in Huntington**, a building that stood until 1860, the site of which is now marked with a sign.

"The house we dined at in Huntingdon was kept by a Widow Piatt, and was tolerably good.…The whole of this days ride was over uneven ground and none of it of the first quality but intermixed in places with pebble stone."

12) He made a brief stop in **Cold Spring Harbor**, where he encountered people working on building the village's first schoolhouse. Much to the delight of the residents, the president stopped to greet them, and this spot, just off today's Route 25A behind the Fish Hatchery, is marked with a commemorative sign; the schoolhouse is long gone. This stop was not noted in his diary.

A sign marks the spot of Platt's Tavern in Huntington, where George Washington dined on April 23, 1790.

13) Washington continued west, stopping at **Oyster Bay, at Young's place**, a small house that still stands today on East Main Street just past the intersection with South Street, across from the First Presbyterian Church.

"Proceeded seven miles to Oyster Bay, to the House of a Mr. Young (private and very neat and decent) where we lodged."

14) After a night at Young's, on the morning of April 24, he traveled to **Roslyn, where he breakfasted at Henry Onderdonk's house**, which was to become what was for many years a popular restaurant called George Washington Manor (corner of Main Street and Old Northern Boulevard) and is now known as Hendrick's Tavern.

"Left Mr. Young's before 6 o'clock and passing Musqueto Cove [now Glen Cove], breakfasted at a Mr. Underdunck's at the head of a little bay; where we were kindly received and well entertained."

15) While in Roslyn, Washington toured **one of Onderdonk's two paper mills**, and as legend has it, made a sheet of paper. In his diary, Washington mentions a third Onderdonk mill, a seventeenth-century gristmill that still stands today on Old Northern Boulevard. The original 1773 paper mill where Washington visited (the first paper mill on Long Island) was in 1915 replaced with a replica that now sits in Gerry Park. The story goes that while at the paper mill, the paper-making process was explained to him, and then

A twentieth-century reconstruction of the eighteenth-century Onderdonk paper mill that George Washington visited in Roslyn on April 24, 1790, on his way back to New York City.

Washington requested permission to make a sheet of paper. According to the August 1919 issue of *Long Island Life*, Washington "removed his gloves, coat, and hat and went to work. He turned a perfect sheet on which he placed a silver dollar for the employee at the mill to have a glass of spirits. The sheet of paper and dollar were preserved for many years, but what finally became of them was never known." This same mill a century later made the cake boxes for President Grover Cleveland's wedding.

"This Gentleman works a Grist & two Paper Mills, the last of which he seems to carry on with spirit."

Thus ended Washington's tour of Long Island. From Roslyn, he headed back to Flushing and then Newtown, where he got a ferry back to Manhattan. There are twelve distinct sites (places George Washington is known to have stopped) on Long Island associated with his 1790 visit. Interestingly, aside from commenting on the reception, food, and lodgings at his various stops, his diary makes no note of any crowds of people greeting him along the way. The only people he mentions are the proprietors or owners of the taverns, inns, and homes he visited. Instead, he mainly devoted space to describing the soil, the roads, and the terrain on his voyage, much of which was unflattering. However, once he was headed from Flushing back to the ferry in Brooklyn, he lavished praise on the conditions: *"The Road is very fine, and the Country in a higher state of cultivation & vegetation of Grass & grain forwarded than any place also, I had seen, occasioned in a great degree by the Manure drawn from the City of New York."*

Though he was already well liked in 1790, the reverence for Washington that we know today continued to grow after his death at the age of sixty-seven in 1799, just two years after he left the office as president; he might well have visited many more places in his retirement had he lived longer. As his stature grew over the course of the nineteenth and twentieth centuries, there was an increasing affinity for the first president, a culture of "George Washington Slept Here." There was even a comedy movie of that name released in 1942 about a couple who move from the city to the country and buy a broken-down house in which Washington allegedly once slept.

On May 25–27, 1927, the Historical Committee of the Long Island Chamber of Commerce and some invited guests (for a total of fifty people) made a tour of Long Island following the same route taken by George Washington 137 years earlier and stopping at all the places he stopped. Of course, the group did not use horse and carriages, but buses, traveling about five hours per day. Ceremonies with period-costumed residents portraying President Washington were arranged at Sayville, Setauket, Huntington, and Roslyn. In Hempstead, a bronze plaque was unveiled on a building at the site of the tavern where the president stopped. The commemorative tour was a success, and thousands of onlookers including schoolchildren were on the route to watch and cheer on the entourage. President Calvin Coolidge and Governor Al Smith of New York personally endorsed the historic tour, and local newspapers gave it much coverage through articles, editorials, and photographs.

The three Washington sites that are still standing and are publicly accessible are Onderdonk's home in Roslyn (now Hendrick's Tavern), Onderdonk's paper mill (though a twentieth-century reconstruction, located in Gerry Park just off the aptly named Papermill Road), and Sagtikos Manor in Bay Shore. While Hendrick's has a space called the George Room, adorned with numerous portraits of George Washington, its website interestingly does not refer to Washington's historic visit there. Sagtikos Manor was acquired by Suffolk County in 2002 and is a house-museum that offers tours during the summer months. Some of the other locations where Washington stopped or passed through are noted with historical markers, dating to as recently as 2014 in Coram, where a sign was funded by a private foundation dedicated to preserving local history.

An entire book has been written about Washington's tour of Long Island (published by The History Press in 2018; another recently published History Press book covers the Long Island spy ring that Washington helped organize during the Revolution). His presence here, though only for four days, may be lost, but it is definitely not forgotten, its legend continuing to grow with the passage of time. While Washington was a legendary visitor to Long Island, there was one president who was not a visitor, but actually called Long Island his home.

Chapter 20

LOST PRESIDENTIAL PRESENCE

Theodore Roosevelt

I n 1880, a wealthy young man from a prominent New York City family bought a large plot of land just east of Oyster Bay village on the north shore of Long Island with the intention of building a home for himself and his new wife, Alice. Theodore Roosevelt had spent summers in Oyster Bay as a teenager in the 1870s and grew to love the beautiful waterfront community. Plans for his house were scratched when his wife died suddenly after the birth of their daughter in 1884, but within a few months, Roosevelt decided that he still needed to provide a good place for himself and his daughter to live (he did eventually remarry a few years later). Though Theodore Roosevelt was not yet famous when he moved into the house he called Sagamore Hill, he would soon skyrocket first to local and then national prominence. In 1882, he had become a New York assemblyman, and from there, he became police commissioner of New York City, assistant secretary of the navy, a colonel in the Spanish-American War, governor of New York State, vice president, and then president of the United States.

From an early age, "Teddy" Roosevelt was a colorful character, full of life, ambition, and a zest for many subjects. He was an adventurer, hunter, conservationist, politician, and prolific author of books on some of his favorite pastimes. He enjoyed travel and gave hundreds of speeches around the country over the course of his life.

Yet despite his numerous travels, Oyster Bay was the home base to which he always returned. As his prominence grew, his presence on Long Island drew more attention in the newspapers. He gained both national

Sagamore Hill, built in the 1880s, is a National Historic Site.

and local adoration for being a quirky, fiery figure. This was especially true after his return from well-publicized heroics during the war in Cuba when he and his band of Rough Riders stormed a hill in San Juan and caused the Spanish to retreat. A *New York Times* article from September 1898 had a headline that read:

> *ROOSEVELT HOME JUBILEE—The Colonel is Lionized by his Oyster Bay Neighbors and Makes a Speech. There were hundreds of men and women in the audience who do not reside in Oyster Bay. There were delegations of citizens from many neighboring towns….Here gathered during the early hours of the afternoon every man, woman and child of Oyster Bay not bedridden. Almost every one of them is personally acquainted with Colonel Roosevelt and was eager to welcome him and point him out with pride to the throngs of visitors.*

His time as governor brought him further opportunities to speak to the people and spread his unique brand of patriotic love. When he appeared at the cornerstone dedication for the new Nassau County Courthouse in

Mineola in July 1900, a crowd of 2,500 people was on hand to hear his brief but inspiring speech about government.

> *Remember that the public servant will do what the people demand of him. You can stop him if he goes wrong. It will be your own fault if you permit sharp practice, if it is exercised at your expense. The people rule, and as they are or are not determined to have decency in public life, they will see to it. It seems to me that in the dedication of a public building in which is to be transacted so much of the work on which the welfare of the community depends we should think seriously over what it means. Free government is not a gift which can be handed out by celestial powers, but only by hard work under self-government and we must preserve it.*

When he became president, Roosevelt brought Oyster Bay and Sagamore Hill into the national spotlight. It was not just his civilian home, it became his "Summer White House," and he spent a great deal of time there meeting with and entertaining both American and foreign dignitaries. He had a reputation as a good listener but also a good speaker, an honest and blunt man who yet knew how to be tactful as necessary. Roosevelt was gruff and kind at the same time; many people know his famous quote "speak softly and carry a big stick." His legend grew in 1902, when he famously refused to shoot a weak-looking bear while on a hunt. A newspaper cartoonist captured that moment, and shortly after, a Brooklyn candy shop owner decided to create a stuffed bear toy in his honor and call it Teddy's Bear.

In the midst of his first term, President Roosevelt designated September 15, 1902, as a special day for the citizens of Nassau County and the villages of Cold Spring Harbor and Huntington (Suffolk County) to come visit him at Sagamore Hill. The village of Oyster Bay made that day a special holiday. Schools were closed, and arrangements were made to present each of Roosevelt's visitors with a keepsake glass etched with "Sagamore Hill September 1902" and filled with lemonade. The local hotel was packed with Secret Service men and reporters. Between four and seven thousand visitors shook Roosevelt's hand that day! He was indeed a man of the people.

On July 4, 1903, Roosevelt gave a speech at the village of Huntington's 250th anniversary:

> *Mr. Chairman, and you, my fellow citizens, my old-time friends and neighbors, men and women of Huntington: I thank you for having given me the chance of saying a few words to you this afternoon. I want not only*

to join with you in an expression of thankfulness for the nation's mighty past, but to join with you in expressing the resolution that we of today will strive in our deeds to rise level to those deeds which in the past made up the nation's greatness.

A month later, Roosevelt gave his "Strength and Decency" speech to the Society of the Holy Name of Brooklyn and Long Island in Oyster Bay, telling the religious audience:

Remember that the preaching does not count if it is not backed up by practice. There is no good in your preaching to your boys to be brave if you run away. There is no good in your preaching to them to tell the truth if you do not. There is no good in your preaching to them to be unselfish if they see you selfish with your wife, disregardful of others.

It was at Sagamore Hill in 1904 that Roosevelt's peace talks with foreign leaders began, which led to the end of the Russian-Japanese War. When peace was achieved, Roosevelt was congratulated by hundreds of leaders and ordinary citizens alike for his role. One newspaper article explained the scene in Oyster Bay:

While the telegraph wires leading into this little village on the shores of the Sound were humming with congratulatory messages from the mighty ones of the world, the President might have been seen dressed in khaki and carrying an axe, striding down the wooded slope near his summer home….Secretary Loeb arrived at Sagamore Hill for his daily session of executive business with the President. He carried a handbag filled with congratulations….Mr. Loeb found the President half hidden behind a pile of wood.

Chopping wood was a favorite activity. Roosevelt could frequently be found somewhere on his large property cutting down trees and chopping them for firewood or fence wood.

It was exactly this combination of personality features—potent world leader and thinker, yet dedicated outdoorsman and nature lover—that made Roosevelt so popular, such a powerful presence. Mind and body, Theodore Roosevelt loved to stay active, and the press loved to cover stories such as this. He loved to ride around Sagamore Hill on horseback. Americans had never known a leader quite like this.

Visitors on their way to see Theodore Roosevelt at Sagamore Hill in 1908. He received countless visitors during his time living in Oyster Bay.

Roosevelt received thousands of distinguished (and interesting) guests at Sagamore Hill. On a single day in 1904, he was visited by the United States district attorney for eastern New York, the assistant secretary of state, drivers who won the New York to Paris around-the-world auto race (the president listened attentively as the men told of animals they encountered in Siberia), and a man who planned to reach the North Pole via airship.

Roosevelt finished out his first term and was nominated for president in 1904; members of the Republican committee went to Sagamore Hill to notify him that he had been nominated. In his nomination acceptance speech at Oyster Bay, Roosevelt proclaimed, "We have already shown in actual fact that our policy is to do fair and equal justice to all men, paying no heed to whether a man is rich or poor, paying no heed to his race, his creed, or his birthplace." His home served as his campaign headquarters for the 1904 election. His track record over three years as president, and his messages of hope and inclusion, resonated with Americans, and he was elected president for a full term. Nassau County residents gave him 60 percent of their vote and Suffolk residents gave him 57 percent, higher than the statewide average of 53 percent and national average of 56 percent.

Even while president, Roosevelt was active in local Oyster Bay organizations; for example, he was a Master Mason at the Matinecock Lodge on West Main Street (the building still stands, and a plaque marks the significance of the spot). He enjoyed mingling with the locals, never thinking himself above the rest of the population. A 1906 photograph shows Roosevelt on the lawn at Sagamore Hill amid a sea of men in black silk top hats; the caption of the image simply reads, "Roosevelt and neighbors."

As president, he had countless accomplishments, and on the homefront, he was especially active in land protection and conservation. He established the United States Forest Service, led the creation of the first national parks and created U.S. National Monuments under the newly signed Antiquities Act (1906). As time passed and his accomplishments increased, Roosevelt's legend continued to grow. Long Islanders were proud to have this magnificent presence in their midst. And his foreign visitors were impressed with his enthusiasm and knowledge. The Prince of Sweden told a reporter after a visit to Oyster Bay in 1907, "I had no idea he was so versed in our history. He was greatly interested in Swedish affairs and fairly brimmed over with enthusiasm concerning our country."

Roosevelt did not run for a third term in 1908, spending some time on safari in Africa but also continuing to grow his reputation as an adventurous American spirit. In 1910, he became the first president to fly in an airplane—just seven years after the Wright brothers first flew. Come 1912, Roosevelt decided to run for president again, this time as a Progressive after he lost the Republican nomination to William Howard Taft. Sagamore Hill again served as campaign headquarters. On a campaign stop in Wisconsin, an assassination attempt was made against him, but the fifty-page speech in his pocket helped stop the bullet from killing him. He gave the speech anyway, refusing medical attention though the bullet had entered his chest. He started his address to the crowd with: "Ladies and gentlemen, I don't know whether you fully understand that I have just been shot, but it takes more than that to kill a Bull Moose" (one of his nicknames). Roosevelt lost the election to Woodrow Wilson but remained as popular as ever with his Long Island neighbors.

His "retirement" was anything but, and he stayed politically and physically active in the years that followed, going on hunting trips abroad but also giving speeches and spending much time on Long Island. In 1917, he wrote a letter to his son Quentin telling of his latest adventures: "Last week Capt. Tommy Hitchcock asked me over to the Mineola aviation ground, to see our

Left: Theodore Roosevelt giving a speech at Sagamore Hill to a crowd in 1916.

Below: Theodore Roosevelt presenting New York Girl Scouts with some of his family silverware to be melted and converted to cash to purchase comforts for American aviators in France. The girls visited Roosevelt on April 25, 1918, at Sagamore Hill during their summer fundraising campaign.

new motor. It had just been fitted into one of the planes; and Blakeley took me up for half an hour in it—an enjoyable ride."

Theodore Roosevelt died suddenly on January 6, 1919, of a coronary embolism. He was only sixty years old. On January 8, a black hearse carried the president's silk flag–draped casket from Sagamore Hill to Christ Church in Oyster Bay for a simple funeral service. Afterward, the procession headed to nearby Young Cemetery, where the coffin was carried uphill to its final resting place in a plot sixty feet from the top of the hill. Oyster Bay, Long Island, and the entire nation were in both shock and mourning.

Roosevelt's widow, Edith, continued to live in the house until her death in 1948. In 1950, Sagamore Hill was acquired by the Theodore Roosevelt Association; the house was opened to the public in 1953. That year, President Dwight Eisenhower went to Oyster Bay to dedicate Sagamore Hill as a national shrine. In his speech he said:

> *Here was a man who was rounded.…He was a great leader and a great student and a great writer. His "Winning of the West" is today a classic. He was a man who understood his fellow human beings. He understood those things for which they yearned and which they deserved under the principles in which he believed. And he set out by patient work.*
>
> *Nothing was too mean for him to do. Nothing was too difficult for him to tackle. There was no one of whom he was frightened as he started to do them. And he had the stamina, the courage, the persistence to carry through.*
>
> *I think that along with the dedication of this house today, if each of us could dedicate himself to attempt to emulate Theodore Roosevelt in his consideration for what we so futilely call "the common man" for want of a better word—that if we could emulate the devotion of that American citizen to all citizens, if we could have his courage in carrying through, his wisdom in seeing what was right and adhering to the right, then I am quite certain that not only will Sagamore Hill and this house stand as a great monument, but each of us in his own way will build a little monument to America.*
>
> *And that is what, after all, he did. He built a monument to America.*

As Roosevelt had met so many thousands of Long Islanders in his lifetime, for many decades after his death, locals who had seen him in person told stories of their encounters and kept his memory alive. But even with the deaths of the last of those who knew him, Roosevelt's Long Island legacy still looms large today. Roosevelt impersonators have for years been part of many celebrations and commemorations in the area, including at Sagamore Hill on July 4. A statue of the former president on horseback greets visitors to Oyster Bay as they enter town. Young children attend Theodore Roosevelt Elementary School. There are reminders everywhere in Oyster Bay of Roosevelt's presence. One corner of the popular Theodore Roosevelt Memorial Park along the waterfront commemorates his life with a display of rocks bearing plaques explaining their significance in the president's life, and several buildings in town have Roosevelt associations as places he worked or visited. Oyster Bay is still very much Teddy's town. Roosevelt's larger-than-life presence on Long Island may be lost, but so great is his legend that the flame of his memory burns as bright as ever.

Chapter 21

YOUR OWN LOST LONG ISLAND

Long Island continues to constantly evolve and change. Every year, more of its history is lost to the societal and economical wrecking ball. Though this book covers some of the larger-scale places that have vanished over the last hundred years, there are thousands more across the island that have disappeared in just the last few decades alone.

As time passes, trends come and go and once-popular activities fade away. Gone are the drive-in movies and roller-skating rinks of the 1940s and 1950s, for example. The latest sports fad on the island as this book is being written is pickleball, and new courts are being created everywhere. While immensely popular now, in twenty years the sport could trail off and courts could be converted into something else. "Here today, gone tomorrow" is a saying that definitely rings true when it comes to our world.

Hopefully this book will make you want to pay closer attention to your surroundings and take note of change as it happens. Remember, whether we realize it or not, we are all witnesses to history in the making. From Glen Cove to Orient Point, from Far Rockaway to Montauk, we are constantly saying goodbye to the old and welcoming the new. It is only by our collective efforts that we can keep the flame of memory still burning so what is gone lives on nonetheless. That is what I have tried to do in this book, and now it's your turn to contribute!

On the following page, write some of the lost Long Island places or events that you have witnessed. Maybe a favorite restaurant closed or an old abandoned movie theater burned down—it is up to you to pick the lost places that have some personal meaning. Record the name, the location, and the date it was lost so that you will create a permanent record for yourself or for anyone who may pick up and read this book in the future.

ABOUT THE AUTHOR

Born in Queens, New York, Richard Panchyk is the author of fifty-five books, including thirty-five books on Long Island and New York City history from the seventeenth century to the present. His books cover a wide array of fascinating, colorful topics that bring the long-lost past back to life. Lavishly illustrated with breathtaking vintage and current photographs, his books take the reader on a visual adventure of hidden history through time and place, revealing everything from long-lost locales to modern mysteries. Besides *Lost Long Island*, his local history titles include *The Beat of New York*, *Abandoned Long Island*, *Dead Queens*, *Hidden History of Long Island*, *Midtown Manhattan Through Time*, *New York City Skyscrapers*, and *Forgotten Tales of Long Island*.